Silver RavenWolf's

TEEN WITCH KIT

How to assemble your altar

1. Flip the box over so that it is sitting on its front, and the side with the pentacle is uppermost.
2. Lift the lid and fold it over along the crease, so that the cut-out pentacle pops up.
3. Tuck the flap behind the back of the tray in which the book and kit items sit.

Please note: you must **never** put lit candles or incense on the paper altar!

Silver RavenWolf's

TEEN WITCH KIT

Everything you need
to make magick!

Illustrations by
Natasha Melhuish

LLEWELLYN

This book is dedicated to:
The memory of our magickal teachers

Text copyright © Silver RavenWolf and Llewellyn Publications 2000
Illustrations copyright © Natasha Melhuish 2000
Figures used on box cover art copyright © Patrick Faricy/Mason Illustration 2000
Box cover computer art copyright © Anthony Duke 2000
This edition copyright © Eddison Sadd Editions 2000

First Edition
First printing 2000

Library of Congress Cataloging-in-Publication Data
RavenWolf, Silver, 1956–
        Silver RavenWolf's teen witch kit -- 1st ed.
                p. cm.
        Includes bibliographical references (p.) and index.
        Summary: Describes modern witchcraft, called the Wiccan religion, and explains how to cast spells and use magickal rituals.
        ISBN 1-56718-554-1
        1. Witchcraft--Juvenile literature. [1. Witchcraft.] I. Title: Teen witch kit. II Title.
BF1566.R33   2000
133.4'3–dc21   99-059442
                                                                                               CIP

Llewellyn Worldwide does not participate in, or endorse, or have any authority or responsibility concerning private business transactions between our authors and the public.

   All mail addressed to the author is forwarded but the publisher cannot, unless specifically instructed by the author, give out an address or phone number.

Llewellyn Publications
A Division of Llewellyn Worldwide, Inc.
P.O. Box 64383, Dept. K554-1
St. Paul, MN 55164-0383, U.S.A.
www.llewellyn.com

AN EDDISON•SADD EDITION
Edited, designed and produced by
Eddison Sadd Editions Limited
St Chad's House, 148 King's Cross Road
London WC1X 9DH

Phototypset in Fontesque and Carmina using QuarkXPress on Apple Macintosh
Printed and produced by Hung Hing Offset Printing Co., Ltd
Manufactured in China

Contents

The World of WitchCraft

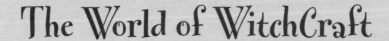

My *Teen Witch Kit* is the first magick package of its kind. It offers teenagers everywhere the chance to look deeply into the mysteries and power of a rapidly growing belief system—the ancient and powerful practice of WitchCraft. The package will introduce you to both the science and the art of a force for good known as Wiccan magick or White magick.

Can WitchCraft help you? Absolutely!

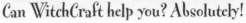

★ Unearth the secrets of good Wiccan magick—and how you can make it!

★ Find out about the many useful ways in which you can incorporate spellcasting into your daily life.

★ Learn all about the magick of the Moon and the ancient magickal practice of Drawing Down the Moon.

★ Create your own sacred space and cast a special magick circle.

My exciting techniques are designed just for you. There is nothing more satisfying than learning to apply magick to all kinds of ordinary, not-so-ordinary, and tricky situations that you find yourself in throughout your teen years. These are very special years, when you will live through all kinds of thrilling challenges and will open up to many new ideas and experiences. There is good and bad to face, and everyone needs a helping hand sometimes—so why not have a little magick on your side!

The *Teen Witch Kit* contains everything you need to whip up over forty enchanting spells and rituals—without having to worry about searching for special ingredients from hard-to-find supply houses or poring over dusty, dull books.

Kit contents

This book that you are reading now, which is all about my spells and rituals for teens. My book introduces the concept of Wiccan magick and provides easy-to-follow instructions for spells and rituals that you can use in your daily life.

A package of essential items that no budding magick-maker can be without, from your own mini-altar to a magickal golden wish cord (see next section for further details of each spellcasting item in the kit).

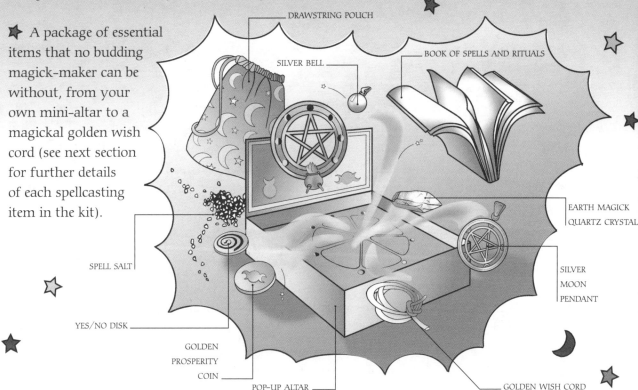

DRAWSTRING POUCH

SILVER BELL

BOOK OF SPELLS AND RITUALS

EARTH MAGICK QUARTZ CRYSTAL

SILVER MOON PENDANT

SPELL SALT

YES/NO DISK

GOLDEN PROSPERITY COIN

POP-UP ALTAR

GOLDEN WISH CORD

First, read through the general instructions in the opening sections of this book. Then just choose whichever spell you would like to do—it really is that easy. My hope is that teens and adults alike will love my super-simple magickal techniques, designed to enhance daily living in a positive way. So, read on, and have some fun!

So, what's this kit really all about?

*H*ey! Have you ever said,

"When I grow up, I'm not going to treat my kids ..."
[just fill in the rest of the sentence]

The only thing is, when lots of teens do actually grow up, they forget what it was like to be younger, and they don't remember what they vowed.

Well, not me. I haven't forgotten, and that's why I wrote this book. I've got four teens of my own, and each day I find myself reliving my teen years through their experiences. Not everything is fair. Not everything goes smoothly. Lots of things are downright scary! And, most importantly, your problems are real. Just because you're a pre-teen, an in-between, or an older teen, it doesn't mean that your problems don't carry the impact of those of an adult. You and I know how tough life can be. You can't just pick up a remote control and switch to another channel if things aren't going too well.

What is WitchCraft?

*W*itchCraft, and specifically Wiccan WitchCraft, is a pro-active, Earth-centered belief system that honors all life. For myself and my children, it has become a living course in miracles. It hasn't always been easy—not because of the belief system itself, but because of other people's perception of it. My children learned early on what discrimination was all about. They discovered that people around them feared anything different, and when people fear something, they act in ignorance.

Whenever anyone asks me, "What is Wicca?" all kinds of things flood into my mind—summarizing Wicca in a few short words is really hard to do. How do I tell someone that my life is filled with love, beauty, joy, harmony, and peace? Will they believe me? Most likely not, because those things seem so hard to attain. So, I could discuss for days what Wicca is or is not, and meanwhile the very best basic answer to the question that I can give is this:

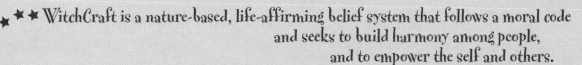

WitchCraft is a nature-based, life-affirming belief system that follows a moral code and seeks to build harmony among people, and to empower the self and others.

We could, in fact, use that statement for a wide variety of beliefs. So what makes those of us who believe in Wiccan magick different? Actually, we aren't so different, but we do celebrate free, individual thought, and don't just follow the crowd without thinking. Wiccan Witches also have a close connection with the world around them—plants and animals as well as people. We commune with Nature, from the sky to the rocks under our feet. To us, every single thing on the Earth is a manifestation of the Divine.

Working together and alone

As with most belief systems, Witches share connections with other practitioners of our faith. The difference lies in the fact that we don't need any kind of central government. Most of the time we do just fine on our own. However, there are times when situations require that we work together, and we usually manage to accomplish this feat and enjoy success right along with the best of them.

The path of any Wiccan is a brave one. You must be willing to learn about yourself (who you really are) and then work on enhancing or improving those qualities that make you an individual. When you reach a confident stage, you can begin helping others—because that's what the Craft is all about— service to humankind. But first, you have to get your own house in order, and that personal house is you.

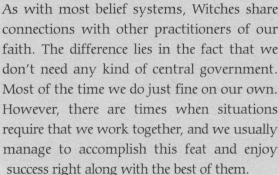
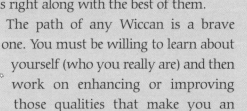

Six simple hints for magick and ritual

I've been practicing magick and ritual since I was a teen myself, and I've learned quite a few helpful hints along the way that I'd like to pass on to you. Granted, you don't have to follow them, but if you do take the time to try them out, I think you'll find that your magickal applications will move along much more smoothly.

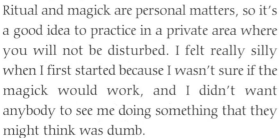 Keep it private

Ritual and magick are personal matters, so it's a good idea to practice in a private area where you will not be disturbed. I felt really silly when I first started because I wasn't sure if the magick would work, and I didn't want anybody to see me doing something that they might think was dumb.

After a while, you won't feel self-conscious any more, but it is still a good idea to keep your activities to yourself. If someone makes fun of you, which people so often do when they understand nothing about something, it is disrespectful and will lower your self-esteem.

Be prepared

Gather everything you need ahead of time, rather than running around looking for something you've forgotten in the middle of a ritual or spellcasting procedure. That way, you don't scatter the energies or the focus of what you are doing.

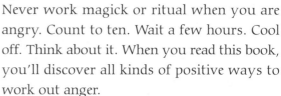 Stay cool

Never work magick or ritual when you are angry. Count to ten. Wait a few hours. Cool off. Think about it. When you read this book, you'll discover all kinds of positive ways to work out anger.

Don't worry

If you mess up a spell or ritual, don't worry about it. Some students are afraid that if they do something wrong, then bad things will happen. Wrong. The walls of the house will not crumble and the basement will not flood. Demons will not crawl out from under the bed and snatch your sister from her crib, Poe's *Tell-Tale Heart* (a short story of his) will not beat beneath the floorboards, nor will a tornado blow through the trailer park and whisk you away to Oz. The worst thing that could happen is that your goal simply won't manifest. Everybody makes mistakes. Acknowledge the error and go on.

★ Don't be afraid

Fear is absolutely your worst enemy. A long time ago, I read a book called *A Course in Miracles* from the Foundation of Inner Peace (currently published through Viking Press). Their motto is:

> *"Nothing real can be threatened.*
> *Nothing unreal exists.*
> *Herein lies the peace of God."*

Study those words and think about them. Write them down on a small card and tack it to your bedroom mirror. Never forget them, they will serve you well.

★ Be honest

Always be honest with yourself and with others. Fibbing only gets you into some very hot water, especially if you work magick. Once you begin to follow the rules of the Craft, you must continue to abide by them.

Whatever you do will come back to you—that's the long and the short of it!

Tools of the trade

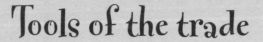

*N*ow that we've talked about what's in the book, let's have a more detailed look at the kit contents, and discuss how you go about using them to make magick.

Kit items

Altar Turn the *Teen Witch* kit box into your personal altar by following the simple instructions on page 2 of this book. The eight phases of the Moon are shown on the outside of the pentacle to remind you of the eight paths to a Witch's power. An altar is a central feature of a Witch's magick-making tools and yours is so convenient because it is small, light, and portable. Place objects connected with your spells on the altar or around it. **Never** put lighted candles or incense on the altar; place them in holders at the side.

Magickal pouch The perfect way to store your magickal goodies! This decorated cotton pocket is designed to hold anything you desire, including some of the magickal items in this kit. Witches often empower items and then place them in a pouch for safekeeping until the spell manifests. When you have received your desire, de-magick the item and start some new magick!

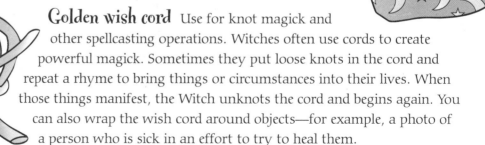

Golden wish cord Use for knot magick and other spellcasting operations. Witches often use cords to create powerful magick. Sometimes they put loose knots in the cord and repeat a rhyme to bring things or circumstances into their lives. When those things manifest, the Witch unknots the cord and begins again. You can also wrap the wish cord around objects—for example, a photo of a person who is sick in an effort to try to heal them.

Silver Moon pendant Wear this around your neck for both protection and good luck! Your pendant features a pentacle (magickal symbol) in the form of a five-pointed star called a pentagram—the symbol of our beliefs. At each of the five points of this pentagram is a crescent Moon—another powerful magickal symbol.

Silver bell Cleanse your room or call up the spirits by ringing this magickal little bell. Ringing the bell three times stands for starting a ritual or for a pause needed in a ritual or spell. Ring the bell four times to call a quarter (see page 40). Ring the bell seven times to call up a spirit, a God or Goddess, or a deceased loved one.

GOD SYMBOL

GODDESS SYMBOL

Golden prosperity coin Use this specially designed coin for prosperity magick. It carries the symbol of the Goddess on one side, and the symbol of the God on the other.

Earth magick quartz crystal Work with the energies of the Earth to develop psychic power or use in meditation. Crystals have the ability to amplify energy. To activate your crystal, hold it under clear, running water for a few minutes. If you can, leave the crystal outside under a Full Moon for at least five minutes. Then, hold it in your hands and ask Spirit (the general guiding energy of the universe; more details are found on page 21) to bless the energies of the crystal as well as yourself. The crystal is now ready for work!

If you lose your crystal, don't panic or get upset. Sometimes, when a crystal thinks it has done all it can, it decides to find a new home—with or without our help. Or they will leave for a while, and then come back later, you never know— that's the fun of working with Earth crystals! To care for your crystal, hold it under running water or under the light of the Full Moon once a month.

Yes/no disk Use for my simple divination technique. The divination coin in this kit is embossed on each side with a sacred spiral symbol and a rune symbol. One side of the coin means "yes" and the other means "no." Most Witches perform some type of divination before they do any magickal work. To know whether or not you should go ahead with a spell that you plan to do, simply close your eyes, ask if the spell should be done, and then flip the coin.

Don't worry if your answer is 'no.' Spirit sometimes knows better than we do what is best for us. Maybe you only have to wait until the correct Moon phase—check again at a later time and then perhaps you can proceed. The coin can also be used in other types of spellcasting shown in this book.

Spell salt Scatter this as you make your magick. Salt has long been used in folk magick for its purifying, preservative energies.

You might also want to use:

Anointing oil Use any oil that is safe to put directly onto skin (read instructions on the bottle carefully first). Place a tiny dab in the center of your forehead before doing your daily devotions or beginning magickal work to cleanse your mind and spirit. You can also use oil to anoint various objects.

Incense sticks and burner These are easy to find in all kinds of shops. Take care with this, as with any burning object, and place it on a safe and stable surface where it won't ignite any other things you might have lying around! Incense is considered a gift to the gods and is used by Witches to cleanse and consecrate the area in which they are working.

A little background information ...

During the time of the Witch persecutions, a practitioner of the Old Ways could not have an altar in his or her home. Some altars were kept outside, far from the house but in walking distance of the homeowner. Going outside, however, meant the danger of being discovered. It is here that the practice of using a living body as an altar may have begun. Despite what Hollywood horror films would have us believe, this doesn't mean our ancestors killed anyone. It just means that a person would lie on the ground and become the altar. When the ceremony was over, there was no altar to hide. The person just got up and walked away.

The power of the elements

The basic tools on most Wiccan altars consist of representations of the elements (Earth, Air, Fire, and Water) and some sort of lighting to see by (such as candles, known as "illuminator candles"). There won't be enough room on your kit altar for all the things you'll collect for your spells. Instead, you can place your altar on a table, bureau, or whatever, and make it the focal point of your magick setup, placing objects around it. You can even take your altar outdoors. Witches love to work outside so that they can be as close to the elements and Spirit as possible.

Today, many Wiccans also add a statue or a picture of a deity between the illuminator candles. We've provided pictures on your altar for you, but if you would like an additional picture or statue, that's fine too. The center of the altar can be left empty, unless you are doing a specific ritual where you wish to place an object with special significance in the center.

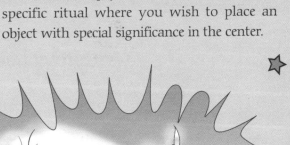

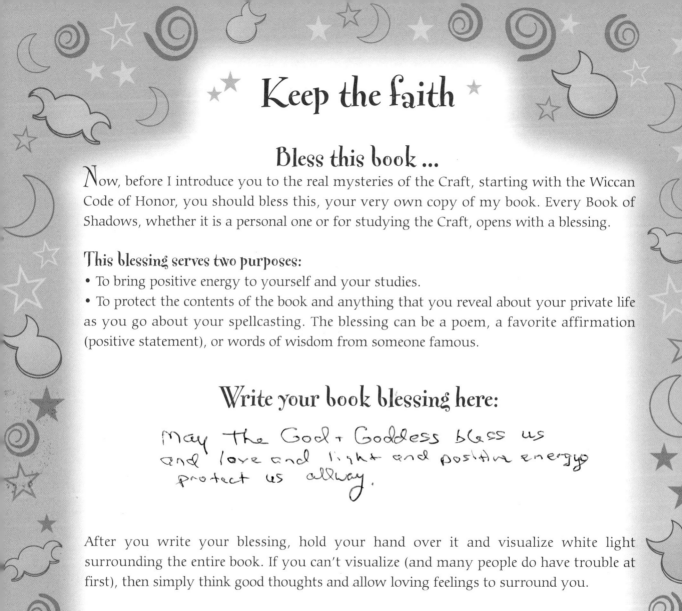

Keep the faith

Bless this book ...

Now, before I introduce you to the real mysteries of the Craft, starting with the Wiccan Code of Honor, you should bless this, your very own copy of my book. Every Book of Shadows, whether it is a personal one or for studying the Craft, opens with a blessing.

This blessing serves two purposes:
• To bring positive energy to yourself and your studies.
• To protect the contents of the book and anything that you reveal about your private life as you go about your spellcasting. The blessing can be a poem, a favorite affirmation (positive statement), or words of wisdom from someone famous.

Write your book blessing here:

May the God + Goddess bless us
and love and light and positive energy
protect us allway.

After you write your blessing, hold your hand over it and visualize white light surrounding the entire book. If you can't visualize (and many people do have trouble at first), then simply think good thoughts and allow loving feelings to surround you.

Once you have blessed this book you are completely ready to enter into the art and science of Wiccan WitchCraft!

Wiccan WitchCraft explained

Welcome to my world—the power and enchantment of WitchCraft!

During the 1970s, the Council of American Witches adopted a document entitled "Principles of Wiccan Belief." This contained thirteen statements that attempted to define the underlying belief system of Wiccan WitchCraft. Obviously this cannot take into account all the subtle shades of belief and practice, but it has served as a useful, simplified starting point for the public and for new practitioners alike.

Now, at this point you're probably saying, "Why do I have to read this stuff? It's so boring!" Well, to some extent, I agree with you. However, I learned long ago that if you don't know the rules, you look like an idiot when someone starts to ask you questions, so bear with me while we work through this section. If you are determined to accept the practice of WitchCraft into your life, you need to know your own history. So here goes, the thirteen statements of belief.

1. We practice rites.

We practice rites (small parts of rituals) to attune ourselves with the natural rhythm of life forces marked by the Moon phases and the seasonal quarters and cross-quarters.

2. We recognize that our intelligence gives us a unique responsibility toward our environment.

We seek to live in total harmony and ecological balance with Nature, offering fulfillment to life and consciousness within an evolutionary concept.

3. We acknowledge a depth of power far greater than is apparent to the average person.

Because this is far greater than any ordinary power, we sometimes give this force the name "supernatural." However, we see this power as lying within that which is naturally potential to everyone.

4. We conceive of the Creative Power in the universe as manifesting through polarity—as masculine and feminine—and that this Creative Power lives in all people.

We hold that this power functions through the interaction of the masculine and feminine. We value neither above the other, knowing each to be supportive of the other. We value sexuality as pleasure, as the symbol and embodiment of Life.

5. We recognize both outer worlds and inner, or psychological, worlds.

Inner worlds are sometimes known respectively as the Spiritual World, the Collective Unconscious, the Inner Planes, and so on. We see in the interaction of the outer and inner dimensions the basis for paranormal phenomena and magickal exercises. We neglect neither dimension for the other, seeing both as necessary for our fulfillment.

6. We do not recognize any authoritarian hierarchy.

Though we do honor those who teach, respect those who share their greater knowledge and wisdom, and acknowledge those who have courageously given of themselves in leadership.

7. We see religion, magick, and wisdom-in-living as united in the way one views the world and lives within it.

This is our world view and philosophy of life, which we identify as WitchCraft or the Wiccan Way.

8. Calling oneself "Witch" does not make a Witch.

But neither does heredity itself, nor the collecting of titles, degrees, and initiations. A Witch seeks to control the forces within him/herself that make life possible to live wisely and well, without harm to others, and in harmony with Nature.

9. We acknowledge the central role of the affirmation and fulfillment of life.
We believe that it is this principle, as part of a continuation of evolution and development of consciousness, that gives a real meaning to the universe we know, and to our personal role within that Universe.

10. Our only animosity toward Christianity, or toward any other religion or philosophy of life, is ... to the extent that these institutions have claimed to be "the one true right and only way" and have sought to deny freedom to others and to suppress other ways of religious practices and belief.

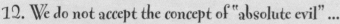

11. We do not feel threatened by debates on the history of the Craft, the origins of various terms, or the legitimacy of various aspects of different traditions.
We concern ourselves with our present and our future, acknowledging that past, present, and future is a matter of individual perception.

12. We do not accept the concept of "absolute evil" ...
... nor do we worship any entity known as "Satan" or "The Devil" as defined by Christian tradition. We do not seek power through the suffering of others, nor do we accept the concept that personal benefits can be derived only by denial to another.

13. We work within Nature for that which is contributory to our health and well-being.
Not bound by traditions from other times and other cultures, we owe no allegiance to any person or power greater than the Divinity manifest through our own being. We welcome and respect all life-affirming teachings and traditions. We seek to learn from all and to share our learning. We do not wish to open ourselves to the destruction of Wicca by those on self-serving power trips, or to philosophies and practices contradictory to these principles. In seeking to exclude those whose ways are contradictory to ours, we do not want to deny participation with any person who carries a sincere interest in our knowledge and beliefs, regardless of race, color, sex, age, national or cultural origin, or sexual preference.

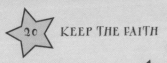

In other words ...

So, what does all this mean when put together and explained in ordinary language? Here goes!

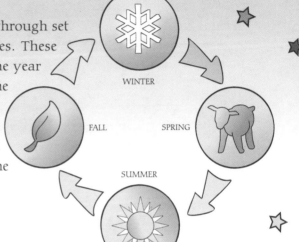

WINTER

SPRING

FALL

SUMMER

Wiccan Witches celebrate Spirit, or God/dess, through set rituals and rites that are like religious services. These usually correspond to set days throughout the year and follow either the phases of the Moon or the seasons of the planet. Instead of holding rituals in special buildings, Witches often meet in the relaxed atmosphere of their own homes, which helps to bring them closer to Spirit and turns the rituals into a community activity.

Right and wrong

Through Spirit, we have knowledge of what is right and what is wrong. We know that it is our responsibility to protect our planet and all the life on it by living in harmony with every life force we encounter.

Witches respect all life—a bug, a weed, a tree, a tiger, or even that classmate of yours. All kinds of life force must survive in order for us all to evolve in a complete way. Witches work with Nature, rather than against it.

Witches do not kill animals (or people), drink blood, or any of that yucky stuff you see in movies. It's amazing just how many people wrongly assume that Witches do this—and of course are horrified—yet accept war without a blink of the eye. Methinks that sometimes the human mind has a rather twisted collective perception of the world.

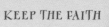

The power of the mind is an incredible thing

Sadly, we've suppressed much of our potential mindpower over the centuries. Buried deep in our underused minds lie all kinds of amazing secret powers—extrasensory perception (ESP), clairvoyance, remote viewing—call it what you will. We all have this kind of power, but most ignore it, and some actively fear it. Spiritual guides such as Witches work to strengthen these natural gifts in others as well as in themselves. Everyone and everything is equal. Ego should not be an issue.

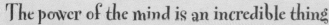

What about God?

Witches do believe in God, but one with two sides—masculine and feminine, also known as the Lord and Lady. Combined, they make up God. "Spirit" is another term that Witches use for God. We believe that God/dess is the supreme power and that no human or group of people is more powerful than God/dess.

This approach comes from the fact that Witches recognize the male and female properties of everything and respect men and women equally. Also, having sexual relations with another person is not a "bad" thing, but it should flow from love, not lust, and carries with it serious responsibilities.

We believe that seen and unseen energies exist in the world. We value the mind just as much as we value the physical world. When we talk about The Collective Unconscious, we mean the psychic connections between people, plants, animals, insects, and Spirit. We believe that religion, the power of the mind, magickal applications, wisdom, and faith in Spirit work together, not separately. We try to be aware at all times of what goes on in the world, and to keep an open mind as much as possible.

Our Inner Planes

The Inner Planes is how we describe the power of our minds. We as Witches recognize that the techniques of paranormal phenomena and magickal application begin in the mind and burst into reality in the world around us. In other words, to think a thing is to create a thing.

Many schools of belief feel that they need to have a central government that dictates rules to its followers. Wicca does not have a central government—each group is self-governing. We do, however, have wise, inspirational, and much-respected teachers and leaders.

Whom do we respect?

We respect the accomplishments of those that practice other faiths, but we are not impressed by people just because they are famous or wealthy. Witches respect all religions on the face of the planet, and respect every individual's right to practice a positive faith. We do not teach our mysteries to fools, and we will exclude people who we feel are either self-destructive or who we feel have the potential, or a history, of hurting others. You'll find that most Wiccan groups screen prospective members.

The way to earn our respect is through admirable personal behavior and actions toward others. We see people as they really are, not as they wish to be seen. But we don't bully or make fun of anyone—that would just be a sign of our own low self-esteem.

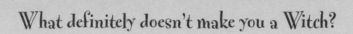

What definitely doesn't make you a Witch?

✴ Reading one book—like this one—and then proclaiming to everyone that you are practicing magick.

✴ Dressing head-to-toe in gothic black clothing and lots of bold jewelry. Some teens were insulted by a similar remark in my book *Teen Witch*, because they liked to dress like this. What you choose to wear is up to you, and if it's black clothes and colorful jewelry, fine. Everyone likes to be a bit avant-garde sometimes, including me! Just realize that there is no uniform that makes you a Witch. Remember—people judge you (although they probably shouldn't) by the way you dress. I wear suits for booksignings and seminars, and jeans and boots in my hometown. Sometimes fitting in with your surroundings is a good idea.

✴ Threatening people with silly curses.

✴ Joining a coven, taking an initiation, and gaining status within the group—yes, even this doesn't make you a Witch.

A question of example

Whether or not you are a Wiccan Witch is down to how you live, how you deal with others, and how you incorporate Wiccan laws into your life. Work to better yourself and your environment, and to help those around you. There is no one right way to practice WitchCraft. The religion is what you make of it.

Don't judge us!

Witches are tired of people in other religions passing judgment and spreading lies about our belief system. This is so often because they themselves are insecure in their own faith. Or perhaps they simply don't see that there are many different paths to enlightenment in our universe. They fear that what they have believed in for many years may not be quite right for them, yet they fear any kind of change. They fight off this fear by trying to force others to see their way of doing things.

Unenlightened people prefer hurting Witches over admitting that people must be free to believe what they want to believe. Witches do not hate people of other faiths, as I've explained. However, when people from these structured groups try to hurt us with lies, gossip, or physical force, they shouldn't be surprised when Witches get upset and fight back. We don't lie down and let people walk all over us. We may bend, but we do not break.

Devil worship ... NOT!

 We do not worship the Devil.

 We don't believe in the Christian Satan.

- We don't follow demonology or demonization.
- We are not interested in working with, in, or through evil.
- We believe that to give evil a name is to give evil power.
- We do not believe that a person gains power by hurting, threatening, or killing someone—that certainly is evil.

Preparing to do magick
What is a spell?

Now that we've gone over the basics, it's time to make some magick. But before we do, we need to talk a little bit about what a spell should look like on paper.

Most people think that a real spell is a little rhyme, throw in a couple of herbs, maybe a candle or two and—*voilà*! A spell! Nope. Spells come in all shapes and forms. Some are big with lots of ingredients, some are small with no tools at all! Many spells are really just darned good advice. There are spells that follow the rules of poetry, and then there are spells that look more like letters written to Deity (these are called testimonials or petitions). Spells can be in the form of meditation or the statement of one thought, uttered a specific number of times (or until you get bored!).

Hidden workings
Spells have two hidden mechanisms that you should be aware of:

1. All spells are designed to change your perception of any situation in a positive way.

2. All spells will change the energy vibrations in yourself and in the environment around you.

How great the impact of a spell is depends on a variety of factors, including your personality, your present environment, and the type of situation or goal on which you are working. This is the reason why one never works negative magick. After all, who wants to become a mean old fuddy-duddy?

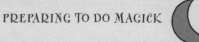

A few of the older spell books on the market recommend weird ingredients. These odd names are really just alternative names for herbs. Spells that called for animal parts and other unusual things followed what is called "The Magician's Herbal Code," which was nothing more than folk names given to various local plants.

Eye of newt

For example, Eye of newt is not the gouged-out eyeball of a creepy-crawly. Eye of newt is *Lavandula angustifolia*, better known as lavender (although I'm not sure where newts come into it) and thought to enhance physical strength and allow the magickal worker to "see" an enemy before they showed themselves. A bit of this herb was put underneath the front doormat or carried in the pocket.

Angustifolia was also added to a black conjure bag (a little black pouch), along with a moonstone, to promote visions. Sometimes it was placed under the pillow to bring about psychic dreams. During the Drawing Down the Moon ceremony, the herb is burned as an incense. I have a Drawing Down the Moon ritual coming up soon in this book, and another a bit later on (see pages 31 and 55), so we'll talk about that a bit more later. You can't eat or drink *angustifolia*—that's a no-no.

In this book you'll find all sorts of spell mechanics so you can get a good overview of spellcasting. Remember, not all spells "look" like the stuff out of a movie. Maybe that's a good thing—after all, Wicca is also called 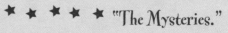 "The Mysteries."

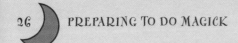

Getting into the right frame of mind

You must be in the right frame of mind before you apply yourself to magick. Getting yourself this way is often referred to as "grounding" and "centering."

Part of any magickal application is learning how to train mind, body, and spirit to work together in order to reach your desires. One of the first magickal techniques I teach my Wiccan students is the exercise of grounding and centering.

This practice comes in handy in a variety of circumstances, including relaxation, preparation for magick or ritual, and removing stress and negativity from the body. Some Wiccan teachers require that the student ground and center before and after any magickal or ritual practice, while others require grounding and centering only after the work. I suggest using the exercise before and after any magickal application while you are still learning.

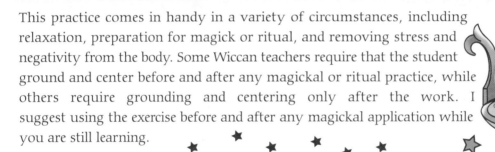

Practice makes ...

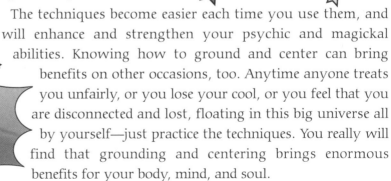

The techniques become easier each time you use them, and will enhance and strengthen your psychic and magickal abilities. Knowing how to ground and center can bring benefits on other occasions, too. Anytime anyone treats you unfairly, or you lose your cool, or you feel that you are disconnected and lost, floating in this big universe all by yourself—just practice the techniques. You really will find that grounding and centering brings enormous benefits for your body, mind, and soul.

Why meditation?

Grounding and centering exercises, also known as meditations,
have several really great uses:

⭐ Grounding and centering before or after any magickal working.

⭐ Incorporating into spells and rituals. For example, you can use the Earth meditation exercise to gain patience by imagining yourself as becoming the most patient individual in the world at the point where you do your visualization. The Fire exercise can be used to spark your imagination—during the meditation, ask Spirit to bring you the creative idea or abilities you feel you need for a particular project. Use a Water meditation to ask Spirit for better relations with your siblings or to learn to share, allowing positive, generous feelings to flow through you. The Air exercise can help you to bend like a willow, without breaking, in times of anger.

⭐ For general relaxation at any time (especially when you are stressed).

⭐ None of the elemental meditations/exercises require any complex physical tools other than yourself, although you can burn incense or light a candle if you like. They reinforce the basic truth that the main tool in any magickal application is yourself.

Grounding and centering exercises

While following these techniques, wear the pendant from your kit. Notice how the rituals are linked to the Earth's four elements and the Moon—all vital to Wiccan Magick.

Air ~ dragon's breath exercise

Face North. Stand straight, shoulders back, arms at your sides. Take a deep breath, close your eyes, and exhale slowly. Inhale and raise your arms slowly over your head, tilting your palms to the sky. Slowly exhale, lowering the arms, and visualizing the sacred dragon's breath leaving your body, taking with it any negativity. (This is the grounding part.)

Now, imagine there is great power resting in your navel. Expand the power out, away from your body, then bring it in slowly, back to your navel. Repeat the whole exercise three times, then take a deep breath and open your eyes.
(This is the centering part.)

Earth ~ tree visualization exercise

Sit on the ground or a comfortable chair. Many Wiccans like to sit under a tree, placing their back against the rough bark of the trunk. If you can, practice at least once using a live tree. You will be amazed at the benefit you receive.

Put your shoulders back, hands on your legs, palms down. Take a deep breath and close your eyes. Imagine you are a tree. Send the roots of your tree down into the dark, rich earth. Down, down, into the soil, soaking up the nutrients of the earth. Down into the molten core of the planet. Don't worry about the heat here—this is the primal energy of Earth—an integral part of you.

Allow all the negativity in your body to course down into the Earth's center. Don't worry about poisoning the Earth with bad vibes. This is simply a way to recycle negative energy into positive fuel. (This is grounding.)

Take a deep breath. Reverse the flow of energy, pulling in positive energy from the Earth up through your roots and into your body. Let this energy flow into your legs, abdomen, arms, shoulders, and head. Breathe deeply and slowly. Feel the energy take root in your abdomen in a calm, airy, glowing ball. Feel yourself filled with a sense of personal power. (This is centering.)

Take another deep breath, and turn your palms over, so that they are facing up, yet resting on your legs. Envision the energy of Spirit coursing down your body from the top of your head to the soles of your feet. Breathe deeply and relax. Slowly open your eyes, feeling refreshed and relaxed.

Water ~ magickal springs exercise

You can practice this visualization while you take a shower. As you wash your hair and clean your body, take a deep breath and allow the water to help you relax. Visualize the water turning into liquid gold energy, scrubbing and cleaning away all the negativity you may have collected throughout the day.

Visualize the water turning into brown muck as it leaves your body and goes down the drain. Keep up the visualization until you can see the water in your mind running clear or gold. (This is grounding.)

Take a deep breath. Now that you are clean, visualize the water hitting your body as liquid silver, transporting the positive energy of the universe into it. Take a deep breath and close your eyes, allowing the water to fill you with a sense of peace and harmony. Raise your arms, if you like, to enhance the energy flow. When you have finished (or the water turns cold!), put your arms down, take one more deep breath, and open your eyes. (This is centering.)

Fire ~ sacred Sun exercise

Sit in a comfortable chair or on the ground in warm weather … whatever, as long as you are directly in the sunlight; but don't get sunstroke!

Put your palms face down on your lap or on the ground. Close your eyes and take a deep breath. Feel the earth/your lap under your hands. Relax and allow all negativity to flow out of your body. (This is the grounding part.)

Now, tilt your head back so that you feel the Sun on your face, but keep your eyes closed (and never stare at the Sun). Turn your palms up so that you feel the Sun on them, too. Take a deep breath, relax, and enjoy the sunlight.

Listen to the sounds of the outdoors. Let your mind float with the sounds. Visualize the rays of the Sun caressing your face, bringing positive, healthy energy into your body. Take another deep breath and allow yourself to relax even more. Thank Spirit for all the wonderful things in your life, and ask that any problems be washed away from you, or that you be given the solutions to solve those difficulties.

When you feel you are finished, take a deep breath and look directly ahead. Take a deep breath, exhale slowly, and then open your eyes. (This is the centering.)

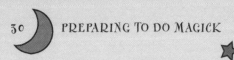

The sacred Moon ~ spirit exercise

Time now to enjoy a grounding and centering technique using the energy of the Moon. In the current Witch culture, the Moon is sacred to the Mother Goddess. There's much more about the Moon later.

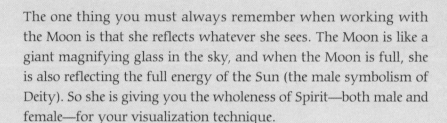

The one thing you must always remember when working with the Moon is that she reflects whatever she sees. The Moon is like a giant magnifying glass in the sky, and when the Moon is full, she is also reflecting the full energy of the Sun (the male symbolism of Deity). So she is giving you the wholeness of Spirit—both male and female—for your visualization technique.

Fill a metal bowl with half a cup of drinkable water and take the bowl outside, under the Full Moon. Set the bowl on the ground, positioned so that the Moon is reflected in the water.

Now stand behind the bowl. Straighten your shoulders, and let your hands fall to your sides. Look up at the Moon and take a deep breath. Exhale slowly. As you inhale, imagine the loving, nurturing energy of the Moon filling your body. As you exhale, concentrate on releasing any negative energy that may have collected inside of you. Once you feel calm and peaceful, slowly raise your arms, palms toward the Moon.

Inhale deeply, asking the Lady of the Moon to fill you with the blessings of the universe. Allow this warm feeling to enter the palms of your hands and course through your body. Exhale slowly. Continue to do this until you feel you are finished. Before you put your hands down, ask the Lady to grant you one wish—then state the wish.

When you have stated your wish, put your hands down slowly. Now pick up the bowl of water, keeping the reflection of the Moon planted on the water's surface all the time. Hold the bowl so that you can continue to see the Moon in the water. Count to seven (this is considered to be a magickal number because each of the Moon's four standard phases are approximately seven days long). Close your eyes, keeping the reflection of the Moon clearly fixed in your mind. Drink the water and, as you do this, imagine the power of the Moon flowing through you, cleansing you, and bringing forth your wish.

After you have drunk the water, put your head back, open your eyes, and look at the Moon again. Thank the Lady for her gifts. Take a deep breath. Congratulations! You have just completed a variation of the technique that Wicca calls **Drawing Down the Moon**.

Be careful what you wish for …

Be really careful about what you ask the Moon to grant because, if the universe feels that the wish is legitimate, it will be given to you. Often, we don't think our wishes through properly, and then when we get them, the responsibility may be rather more than we originally bargained for!

Drawing down the Moon

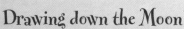

This procedure is one of the most common occurrences in Wiccan WitchCraft. It is where you take the energy of the Moon and pull that energy into yourself. Although you may think this strange at first, consider how you feel when you look at a Full Moon on a clear night in a starry sky. There is a sense of mystery, pleasure, and excitement as you gaze at her luminous face.

Reflected glory

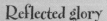

Scientifically, the Moon does affect the universe through gravitational pull, affecting the tides of the sea. So what you feel isn't scary—it's perfectly natural!

Science also tells us that the Moon has no light of her own – she shines because she reflects the light of the Sun. In the Craft, it is believed that the God (the Sun) lends his power to the Goddess (the Moon) so that she can dispense this energy to the Witches (and others) as she sees fit. To Witches, the Moon is like a giant mirror in the sky that boosts any energy sent to it, like a funhouse mirror where you look really big although you may only be four feet tall!

Creating a sacred space

A Witch begins most of their work (magick or ritual) in sacred space. Sacred space is created by cleansing the area with the four elements: Earth, Air, Fire, and Water.

You can use any form of these elements you desire—for example, dirt from your backyard, movement of the air by using a feather, a candle to represent fire, and water from the tap or holy water (see features on Homemade Elements and Making Holy Water, pages 34 and 35).

Indoors or out

Sacred space need not be empty. For example, if you are going to use your bedroom to work magick, there will be lots of stuff in there—from your bed to stuffed animals, sports equipment, school books … whatever. That's okay. You can create sacred space anywhere—indoors or out. However, some elements are harder to use—for example many teens and college students aren't allowed to have fire in their rooms. That's okay, too. Make a pretend candle out of paper and use your imagination. I can't stress enough how careful you should be with candles and fire. Place any candles **next to** your flammable paper altar, **not** on it, and keep some water at hand. Always ask your parents or guardians first for permission to use candles.

"Cleanliness is next to Godliness"

—the old saying is all too true where magickal applications are concerned!

Make a clean start

Although you're going to groan at this part (but it really was time you threw away that two-month-old peanut butter sandwich), you should clean the room thoroughly before you work magick or ritual. Dust, debris, and dirt collect negativity, which may hamper your work. You don't have to clean every single time, but a good once-over each month isn't a bad idea—and your parent or guardian will be amazed! After you have cleaned your room, it's time to create sacred space. Gather your representations of the four elements, thinking creatively and looking at the homemade elements list (page 34) for inspiration. Each element represents a direction, and is often associated with a specific color:

EARTH ~ North ~ Green   AIR ~ East ~ Yellow   FIRE ~ South ~ Red

WATER ~ West ~ Blue   SPIRIT ~ Center ~ White

Get focused

You may want to put a candle at each quarter (quarters of the compass: North, East, South, and West) to help you focus on creating sacred space. How do you know where the candles go? Well … get a compass, stand in the center of your space, and find North. Then locate the other directions and place your candles accordingly. If you aren't allowed to use candles, that's okay. Pick something else to help you focus. It is entirely up to you—that's the beauty of WitchCraft!

Get grounded and get started!

When you feel you are ready to begin, follow these steps:

1 Ground and center like I taught you a few pages back.

2 Pick up your representation of the Earth element and walk in a clockwise direction around the room, sprinkling a little bit of Earth on the floor and saying:

"I cleanse and consecrate this place in the name of Spirit by the element of Earth. May no evil or negativity abide here. So mote it be!"

3 Pick up the Air representation and walk in a clockwise direction around the room, saying:

"I cleanse and consecrate this place in the name of Spirit by the element of Air. May no evil or negativity abide here. So mote it be!"

4 Follow up with your Fire object, saying: *"I cleanse and consecrate this place in the name of Spirit by the element of Fire. May no evil or negativity abide here. So mote it be!"*

5. Sprinkle the water around the room in the same manner, saying: *"I cleanse and consecrate this place in the name of Spirit by the element of Water. May no evil or negativity abide here. So mote it be!"*

Homemade elements

You can use all kinds of things to represent the four elements:

Earth
✢ Dirt from your backyard
✢ Salt—from this kit or your kitchen cupboard
✢ Sand

Fire
✢ Lit candle
✢ Pretend candle made from paper, cardboard …
✢ Picture/image of the Sun
✢ I don't recommend matches because of their sulfur content. Most Witches do not allow sulfur into the magick circle, simply because of the negative association of fire and brimstone from old medieval texts. Sulfur also smells pretty gross.

Air
✢ Movement of the air by using a feather
✢ Incense
✢ The silver bell that comes with your kit—ring it three times to represent Air

Water
✢ Tap water
✢ Sea water, spring water, rainwater
✢ See Making Holy Water (on the opposite page) on creating for yourself the holy water that many Wiccan Witches use.

6. Stand in the center of the room, hold your arms out from your sides, palms down, and say:  *"I ask for the blessings of the Earth upon this sacred space."*

7. Turn your palms up, and say:

"I ask for the blessings of Spirit upon this sacred space."

8. Visualize blue-white light surrounding you and the room. Don't be afraid if you feel a little giddy—that's only natural. You've just welcomed Spirit into your life.

Making holy water

You might like to make some Wiccan holy water for yourself. Here's how:

Fill a glass or a small glass bowl with water. Hold your hands over it and say:

"I exorcise thee, O creature of water,
of all negativity both seen and unseen,
and bless thee in the name of Spirit!"

Imagine a blue-white light filling the water. Take your time. Hold your hands over a small amount of salt and repeat the same words, substituting the word "salt" for the word "water." Envision the same blue-white light covering the salt. Add three pinches of salt to the water, and stir three times. Hold the bowl up at eye level with both hands, and say:

"I cleanse and consecrate this water in the name of Spirit. May
this liquid enhance and purify all that it touches. So mote it be!"

Casting your magick circle

A Witch performs most of their work in the confines of a magick circle. A magick circle begins in your mind and becomes a physical expression of your personal space—a place where you feel protected and safe. This personal space is dedicated to divinity (whether that divinity is the Lord and Lady, an archetype such as the goddess Diana or the god Kernunnos, or even Mary, the divine mother of the Christian belief system).

Most creation myths, in all kinds of cultures, contain the symbolism of the circle. It represents the sacred, infinite dance of life and all that exists in the universe—all time, all possibilities, ever-beginning and never-ending. You will find many references to this symbol in the Craft of the Wise. Witches view the cycle of birth and death as a circular pattern and also stand in a circle when celebrating High Holy Days (together called the Wheel of the Year). The circle is a sacred place where all participants are considered equal. Which is why Witches cast a magick circle to contain their work and raise power.

What type of circle?

Your circle is something that you visualize and bring into being. The circle is not flat and linear, like a two-dimensional circle you might draw on the floor. It should encompass you—above your head and below your feet—like a bubble. Although most Witches cast a circle with the linear motion of their hand or a hand-held tool (such as a wand), they actually visualize a circle rising above and below them.

Make your circle whatever size you want. Most solitary Witches, I've found, cast their circle to match the room size—that way they can move about the room without breaking the circle barrier. Can you cast a circle around things in your room—a bed or desk? You most certainly can. Anywhere your mind can go, the circle will follow—you just have to envision the circle in that way.

How do you do it?

Casting a circle is easy. Every Book of Shadows contains at least one style of circlecasting. Although the basics are often the same, each Witch learns to cast in their own personal way or may follow the way they were taught by an instructor.

In my clan, we begin casting our circle in the North (facing North). Our teachings state that "everything comes from the North," meaning that the North is the seat of stability and prosperity for us. The North Star (when we work stellar magick) is the focus of our practices. The other most common direction to begin with is the East, and many Witches use that direction as a part of their basic approaches. To them, the rising of the Sun denotes beginnings, and the East is the seat of the intellect. In this book, however, I have chosen to use the North. Give it a try, and see what you think. Stand facing the North. Take a deep breath. If you are right-handed, extend your arm and point the index finger of your right hand out away from you toward the ground. (If you are left-handed, use your left index finger.) As you say the circlecasting words given on the right, walk in a clockwise direction around the edge of the room or chosen area, visualizing a leafy green hedge

rising from the ground and encompassing the area in a protective bubble of greenery. Walk the circle three times. The words are:

"I conjure thee, by dragon power,
a circle now around us stands!
I trace the path between the worlds,
A boundary line of gods and man.
Once around I trace the path,
Twice, it turns into a flame.
Three times around, a wall of Fire,
Within whose realm we will remain.
This ground is sacred, consecrated
By the power of Earth and Air.
We conjure Fire to cleanse our hearts
And Waters deep to guard us here.
In the name of She who watches,
In the name of He who stands,
This circle bright is bound around us
While Spirit works its mighty plan.
As above, from crown of heaven,
Now below, it is revealed,
Magic circle, O crystal fortress,
By my words your power is sealed! Blessed be."

Is the circle there even though you can't see it? Absolutely! Eventually, you will learn to sense your circle either by touch, sight, or gut feeling. Every Witch senses energy differently, so don't think that you've failed if you don't "see" anything. The longer you practice, the better you get at sensing the energy. It might take a few months, but remember that kids take to magick a lot faster than most adults because their imaginations are less diluted by social conformity.

A few rules to observe ...

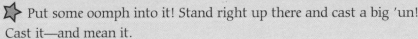

☆ Put some oomph into it! Stand right up there and cast a big 'un! Cast it—and mean it.

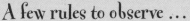

☆ Once you have cast the circle, nothing should break it. If you absolutely must leave the circle area, you will have to "cut a door," much like parting a curtain with your hands. There are many ways to cut a door, but a gentle parting seems to work best for me. When you leave the circle, you should turn and close the opening until you return.

☆ Sometimes you will forget and rush out of the circle— perhaps someone is calling for you. That's okay, it happens. However, walking through the circle lessens its power, and if you do it too many times, it might disintegrate. How many times depends on the Witch, the type of circle, and how strongly it was cast.

☆ Animals and small children do not affect the structure of the circle. Both are considered blessed by the gods.

☆ If someone walks through your circle uninvited, don't make an issue of it. Your consternation will cause more harm than good, so just wait until they leave and fix the damage, or simply recast. No biggie.

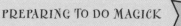
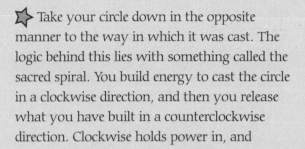 Take your circle down in the opposite manner to the way in which it was cast. The logic behind this lies with something called the sacred spiral. You build energy to cast the circle in a clockwise direction, and then you release what you have built in a counterclockwise direction. Clockwise holds power in, and counterclockwise lets it out. You need walk around only one time, counterclockwise, to take up the circle, holding your finger out and imagining the circle coming back into your hand. Some people take their circle down by using the word "dismiss," but that's sort of a command, and I'm not comfortable with that.

On occasion, you may forget to release the circle, or the quarters (see later on). It's really better if you go back and release all energies. If you don't, nothing terrible will happen, but you may feel wired for a while. Try not to forget next time.

When you want to release the circle, you can choose to put its remaining energy into your favorite magickal tools, your altar, your body, or the universe. If you want to release the energy into an object, draw the circle up by visualizing the energy growing like a ball of light in your hand, then place it on top of the object. If you want to release the energy into the universe, to ask for healing for the planet, hold up your hands, palms to the heavens, and imagine the circle energy melting into the air.

Sealing the circle

Whenever a Witch seals a circle, they say:

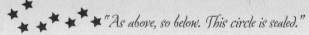 *"As above, so below. This circle is sealed."*

Although there are several meanings to this statement, the one we will concentrate on here is this: What happens in the heavens is reflected on Earth; and what happens on Earth is reflected in the heavens. A Witch "seals" everything they do—much like tying off a sewing project—to keep dangling threads of energy from unraveling.

Calling the quarters

Now that you've learned about casting a magick circle, it's time to move on to a procedure called "Calling the Quarters." Calling quarters means to invite specific energies to enter your circle at the four compass points—North, East, South, and West. (Some people who practice magick use eight divisions: North, Northeast, East, Southeast, etc.)

Quarters are normally associated with the energy of the four main elements, and have other associations, too: totem animals, angels, watchtowers, dragons, winds, deities, and countless other entities.

Using the power of the elements will give you a firm base on which to build your Craft knowledge, while the dragons, for example, will really help you out with your visualization skills. It is the symbol of the fiery and magickal dragon that we have used in our example invocation on page 43.

Not all magickal applications or rituals require quarter calls, and you don't have to call them all the time. Once again, as with so many aspects of this free and individual belief system—the choice is yours.

At one with your planet

When we begin learning how to use the energy of the quarters of a circle, with its links to the compass points and the elements, we are taking our first steps toward learning how the world around us is put together. We seek to use body, mind, and spirit to become one with the universe, getting to know the world around us and looking within ourselves to learn exactly who we are and what it is we wish to become.

How to make that call

There are all kinds of quarter calls. Choose whichever style suits you, and stick with that for a while until you are comfortable with those energies. Quarters are normally called after the circle is cast (and we'll follow that order here), but some Wiccan Witches call the quarters beforehand. In this book we call the four quarters in a clockwise direction—North, East, South, and West. And you can also ring the silver bell that came with your *Teen Witch* kit four times to call each quarter.

The best way to begin using quarter calls is to memorize them, and stay with the same call until you can do it in your sleep. When you call a quarter, you invite specific energies into your circle to help you with your work. Not only do you verbally call the energies, but you visualize them as well. You feel the energy as it comes into the circle and, while you are calling, you become that energy. When students begin the study of Wicca, they may fear energy because it is something they can't normally see. They quickly learn to feel the energy, and then realize that nothing scary lurks there.

The quarter calls

There are three parts to any quarter call:

1 The words you say (or the sounds you make).
2 The motions you make with your hands or body movement.
3 The visualization you create.

The three are usually done all at once. For example, to open the North quarter you might hold your hands at your heart and then, while saying the words, open your arms slowly, as if opening a door. If you can, speak the calls aloud. The vibration of your voice creates energy and concentrating on speaking the words helps you—and any others in your circle with you—to be more focused. While you are speaking the words and opening the quarter with your hands, you will also be visualizing the quarter energies. Some Witches use tools, such as a wand, to call the quarters, but you don't necessarily need tools to practice magick, and your hands are more powerful than a wand will ever be.

Where do quarters fit in with spells?

Once you have cast the circle and called the quarters, you are ready to begin your ritual or spellcasting. Although you may not work with the quarters again throughout the ritual, their energy continues to move into and around the circle. Don't worry, there aren't all kinds of other unwanted energies in there with you— unless a person filled with negativity steps into the circle —so be assured that only the energies you want are there, keeping you safe and protected.

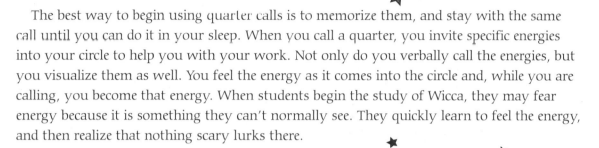

Some spells and rituals employ energies at all the quarters; some at only one. Again, this depends entirely on you and the focus of what you are doing. For example, if you are trying to raise your grades, you might ask the East quarter to bless you with clear thinking during some part of the ritual.

Closing the quarters

To call the quarters, we opened the door. To release them, we shut the door. As with the magick circle, we set things up running clockwise, and then release them going counterclockwise. So, to release the quarters, we start with the West, move to the South, then to the East, and finally to the North quarter. Quarters are normally closed before you release the circle.

For the movements we make to release, we might begin with our arms open, and then, as we say some closing words aloud, slowly close our arms until our hands are clasped over the chest. At the same time, we would be visualizing the energies leaving the circle. If you can't see them in your mind, then concentrate on feeling them go. If you had candles burning, you might put them out at the end of your release to signify visually that those energies have left the circle. Try ringing your silver bell seven times as you release each quarter.

Dragon power

Dragons, in their own way, are real—whatever you invent with your mind can become a reality—this is one of the main principles of WitchCraft. No, a big green dragon is not suddenly going to appear at your dining room table and convince all of your family that you have a secret pact with the Devil.

The energies of the lovable dragons are very much there, however, and you will really enjoy working with them. Oriental mythology celebrates the dragon as a creature that brings good fortune and strength, and Wiccan Witches think so, too.

Dragon quarter calls

The dragon quarter calls work just like any other kind of magickal invocation. Stand at the associated quarter (North, East, or whatever), say the words shown below, and think about the dragon that you are inviting to assist you. Before you say the following invocation, or any other magickal invocation, ring the silver bell four times.

"Power of ancient dreams, dragon of the mysterious North, come forth, O guardian of the Earth. Stand your watch throughout this rite. Let the North Star crown your brow. Hear this call of the Witch. Let my words draw you near. Lock the gate that none may pass, unless they come in love and trust. Blessed be.

"Power of ancient dreams, dragon of the mighty East, come forth, O guardian of the Air. Stand your watch throughout this rite. Let your wings protect us! Hear this call of the Witch. Let my words draw you near. Lock the gate that none may pass, unless they come in love and trust. Blessed be.

"Power of ancient dreams, dragon of the mighty South, come forth, O guardian of the Flame. Stand your watch throughout this rite. May your fiery breath cleanse our work. Hear this call of the Witch. Let my words draw you near. Lock the gate that none may pass, unless they come in love and trust. Blessed be.

"Power of ancient dreams, dragon of the mighty West, come forth, O guardian of the Waters. Stand your watch throughout this rite. May your sweeping waters flow to bring protection all around us. Hear this call of the Witch. Let my words draw you near. Lock the gate that none may pass, unless they come in love and trust. Blessed be."

To release the dragon quarters when you have finished your ritual, walk counterclockwise, stop at each quarter position, and bid the dragons farewell. Thank them for helping you with your ritual.

[written by David Norris © 1999]

About your altar

Most religions, past and present, feature a kind of altar as an anchoring centerpiece in a ritual celebration. And, on a practical note, it's a flat surface where you can put your sacred stuff. Any item you use (even your toothbrush) eventually carries your energy, which builds over time. It's the same with your altar, and the more you work at your altar, the stronger its positive power becomes.

Respect!

Altars can be temporary or permanent, erected inside the home or out. Choose any flat surface, as long as you respect that area and keep it clean. No dirty socks or empty soda cans—trash and dust just collect negativity.

The box of your kit folds into a handy, portable altar that you can place on your chosen flat surface. The design on the left side of the pop-up pentacle stands for the Goddess, and the design on the right stands for the God. The eight phases of the Moon (depicted around the pentacle) also correspond to the eight paths of Wiccan power.

You will need:

* Incense of your choice
* Salt in a bowl (Earth)
* Silver bell or a feather (Air)
* A red candle (Fire)
* Water in a bowl (Water)
* Scented oil of your choice

Activating your altar

Before using your altar, you must cleanse, consecrate, and activate it. Most Witches do this by passing a representation of the four elements over the surface, then sealing those energies with oil or perfume. Set up your kit altar, and arrange the items beside it. That way, you can cleanse, consecrate, and activate the whole lot at once.

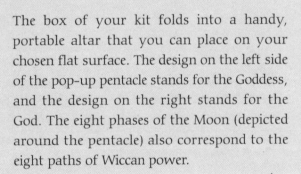

What you do

Light the incense and begin by holding your hands over the items and saying:

*"Powers of the land
Powers of the sea
Powers of the heavens
Power of the Lord
Power of the Lady
Bless these things for me."*

Hold your hands there until they tingle or begin to feel warm. One at a time (salt first, then the feather or bell, then the lit candle, and finally the bowl of water), pass each item over the altar in a clockwise, circular motion. Be very careful with any lit items and keep them away from your paper altar. Now hold your hands over the altar and ask your version of divinity to lend power to the altar and your magickal workings. Witches often say, "In the name of _____" and say the name of the deity or energy aloud.

To seal the center of your altar, use your index finger, anointed with the scented oil, to draw any of the symbols shown in the box on the right over the altar.

Activating symbols

△ This is the ancient symbol for an altar. The triangle represents the divine feminine principle and the horns are associated with the divine masculine principle.

+ The equal-armed cross is used to seal just about any magickal activity. Its four points stand for the four elements, the Moon's four phases, the four archangels, the four winds, and the four cross-quarter holidays (Beltane, Lammas, Samhain, and Candlemas) or the four quarter holidays (Spring Equinox/Ostara, Summer Solstice/Midsummer, Fall Equinox/Mabon, and Winter Solstice/Yule).

◎ This spiral—also found on your kit's yes/no coin—symbolizes the cycle of death and rebirth. To draw power into the altar, begin drawing your spiral clockwise from the outer edge into the center of the altar.

☆ The pentagram is the symbol most often associated with magick, which is why it appears on your special kit pendant. Its primary meaning is that of life and health. The five points of the star stand for Earth, Air, Fire, Water, and the spirit of humankind (the top point). The circle represents how the energies of the world and humans are encompassed by divine protection.

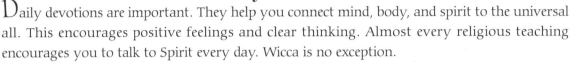

Daily devotions

Daily devotions are important. They help you connect mind, body, and spirit to the universal all. This encourages positive feelings and clear thinking. Almost every religious teaching encourages you to talk to Spirit every day. Wicca is no exception.

Practicing daily devotions can be a formal or informal process. Many magickal people talk to Spirit at least once a day while sitting by their altar at home. Others take a private walk in the morning or evening, speaking to Spirit as they go, or practice their devotions as they drift off to sleep at night. Some recite a favorite poem or other passage to connect them to divinity. Try the following for size:

Devotion of the elements

Take a deep breath and exhale slowly. Feel your feet connected to the earth. Hold your arms in the shape of a chalice, palms slightly tipped to the sky (the Goddess position). Look at the sky or close your eyes (whichever is most comfortable), and say:

"Each day I swim in the cauldron of life and transformation, reaching out for my destiny. May the Lord and Lady grant me the stability of the Earth, the intelligence of the Air, the passion and courage of the Fire, the positive transformation of the Water, and the expanding love of the universe. So mote it be."

Lower your arms. Take another deep breath and exhale slowly.

Daily devotion of the ancestors

The idea for this devotion comes from writer Ray Malbrough. He teaches that your ancestors are very important in understanding your place in life—how you got here, and how energy that flows into you from the past will direct you toward the future.

To practice this devotion you should do some research on your family history. Collect pictures and talk to your relatives. What was the world like for them? What circumstances changed and enhanced their lives? Before we begin, let's not confuse honoring those who went before us with worship. They weren't and aren't gods. They have good and bad traits.

Most magickal people believe that those who have passed away are able to assist the living. This isn't a scary thing. If Grandma loved you before she left this world, she isn't going to turn into a rolling-eyed monster in her afterlife. It's perfectly okay to ask Grandma for a little positive energy to help you when you've got a major problem.

Once you have investigated your family history, write down your ancestors' names and their relationship to you on a piece of paper. Light a purple or white candle (or use a representation of a candle), and say something like this:

*"I honor those who have gone before me.
May Spirit bless my ancestors.
I honor my Mother [name]
I honor my Father [name]
I honor my Grandmothers [names]
I honor my Grandfathers [names]
I honor my Great-grandparents [names if possible]
Time is not linear
Time weaves and undulates
All paths are circular to Spirit.
Bless those that have gone before me
And those that will come after me.
So mote it be."*

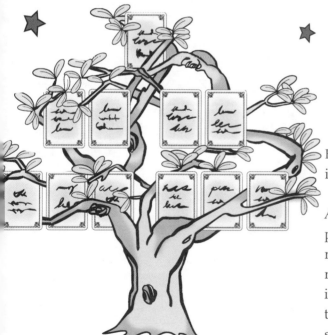

Feel free to add any friends or pets to your list—in fact, anyone you like.

What if you don't like someone on that list? Ask Spirit to bless them anyway—they probably need it more than the others! If recalling those who have died is painful, remember that they are always with us, even if only in memory. Honoring them is a way to turn grief into positive energy and experience a sense of connectedness with the universe.

Let the magick begin ... Spells for every occasion

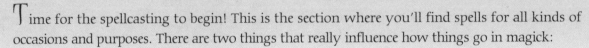

Time for the spellcasting to begin! This is the section where you'll find spells for all kinds of occasions and purposes. There are two things that really influence how things go in magick:

1. Our Lady, the Moon.
2. The days of the week.

So we've divided the spells section that follows into these two areas, with plenty of spells and magickal advice in each. Here goes!

Moon magick

Witches use the energy of the Moon in three ways:

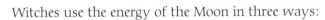

- As a symbol of the Goddess.
- As a catalyst for raising energy.
- To find the right moment for certain types of ritual and magick.

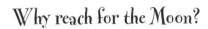

Why reach for the Moon?

We've already talked a bit about the importance of the Moon, under Grounding and Centering exercises. So you know that the Moon affects the universe—including you and your body—through gravitational pull.

Witches believe that their power is given a huge boost when they acknowledge the energy of the Moon. And you know that our Moon—the Witches' Lady Goddess and

principle of female divinity—shines because it reflects the light of our Lord, the Sun (male divinity)*. In the Craft of the Wise, the Sun lends his power to the Moon so that she can dispense this energy to Witches (and others) as she sees fit.

More and more people are discovering how the Moon and its different phases affect our feelings, our decision making and all aspects of

*Choose your own names to represent whichever face(s) of the God or Goddess you wish to be your patron deity.

our lives. The Moon is the key that unlocks the door, whether we are talking about when to plan an event or reach a goal, or when to cast a spell. When you begin magick-work, you'll also discover lots of astrological links. You'll see how different astrological signs affect the Moon and the Moon, in turn, affects you and me.

Most Witches use a magickal almanac to determine the Moon phase and when the Moon visits each astrological sign. (If all this seems confusing, don't worry. Work with the phases first, then progress to the more

challenging idea of the Moon in the signs.) Once the position of the Moon is determined, the next step is to plan your magickal work. If you don't have a magickal almanac, check your local newspaper under the weather section—you'll find that the Moon phase is usually posted there.

Moon timing

Moon phases have been used to measure time since the days of the ancients. In the Craft, the phrase "from Moon to Moon," means from when a spell was performed at a specific Moon phase until the following repeat phase. Though Witches often mean "from Full Moon to Full Moon," the phrase may refer to any other Moon phase.

If what they have worked for does not happen by one full Moon cycle (twenty-eight days) most Witches try again, reworking the spell. I know it's frustrating having to wait for an outcome, but it just has to be done sometimes. This does not mean that you've failed. Remember, magick travels the path of least resistance. If there are obstacles, the energy will move off in a different direction that you may not have anticipated. When you are first learning the Old Ways it is natural for spells to take a little longer. Don't be surprised if it takes several Moons to accomplish your goal.

A little science

✰ Our Moon reflects the Sun's light—that's why it appears to shine.

✰ Our Moon moves around the Earth, spinning as it goes.

✰ The Moon's different phases—how much of its lit surface we can see—depends on its position in relation to the Earth.

✰ The Moon takes about twenty-eight days to go right around the Earth. It takes exactly the same time to revolve on its own axis. This means that the same side of the Moon is always facing the Earth.

✰ In Moon lingo, there are four quarters—New Moon, Half Moon/first quarter, Full Moon, then Half Moon/last quarter.

✰ There are eight phases—the four quarters plus four in-between stages where the Moon is waxing and waning, producing those lovely crescents.

Planning your Moon magick

The complete cycle of the Moon is rather like a miniature version of any project you or I might undertake. First there is a beginning/planning, then comes the main task of the work itself, followed by the results of that work and what you will reap for all your time and trouble. Finally, you get to rest after your labors—until you decide to start a new project, that is!

The Moon's quarter measurements also relate to the Goddess. She is born at the New Moon, becomes the Maiden during the second quarter, maturing into the Mother during the third quarter, and grows old and wise as the Crone at the fourth quarter, finally passing into death and being born anew with the following new Moon. Follow this logic to plan your magick and you can't go wrong.

Here's how to plan your magick according to the Moon's phases.

(DARK MOON)
NEW MOON
WANING
WAXING
PHASES OF THE MOON
MOON
MOON
FULL MOON

The New Moon—This is the time to begin a project/new phase in your life etc.

The Waxing Moon—This is the time to build on what you already have.

The Full Moon—A perfect time to undertake anything at all.

The Waning Moon—The time to finish a project or undertaking.

The Dark of the Moon (sometimes called the Balsamic Moon or Waning Crescent)—The time to banish anything or a time of rest.

The Dark of the Moon

Okay, so the Dark of the Moon really isn't a quarter, but it is the last of the eight phases, and I added this information for you because sometimes, like it or not, we need that Dark Moon to get rid of bad habits or to remember to take a break. The Dark of the Moon is a time of transition between the last quarter of the Full Moon and the New Moon. It's a great time to curl up with your favorite book, take a bubble bath, write poetry, paint a picture, play with your pets, read to your little sister (don't groan), play a video game, or watch your favorite movie.

The difference between the waxing and waning Moons

If you want to impress your boyfriend (or girlfriend) while you stand under that star-studded summer sky, here's the key to remembering which quarter is which:

If the Moon looks like a big "D" in the sky, then it's waxing (growing bigger). Think of the word "double." If the Moon looks like a "C" in the sky, then it is waning (getting smaller). Think of the word "contracting." (Reid, Lori, *Moon Magic*, Crown Publishers, NY, NY, 1998.)

"Moon Void of Course"

Now, this Moon-jargon phrase refers to something slightly different. The Moon passes through the twelve signs of the Zodiac as it makes its twenty-eight-day journey around the Earth, spending a couple of days in each sign. When it passes out of one sign, just before it enters the next, this stage is called a Void Moon. This takes place every few days and lasts between a few seconds to a couple of days. Witchie rule No.1 is NEVER attempt anything of any importance at this time—it will only fail. Think of it like this—The Moon is resting and she's got her answering machine off. Take a break yourself, as you do when the Dark Moon comes, and try her phone again later.

About the only way you are going to know when the Moon is Void of Course is if you use a magickal almanac, subscribe to a monthly horoscope magazine, or can find a computer program that tracks Moon voids.

The Goddess Moon

This is the symbol of the Goddess Moon. In Wicca, the Goddess is called "She with many faces and many names," and is often shown with a feature—such as a crescent on her head—that links her with the Moon. She is also linked with the cauldron —another important symbol of the Female Divine principle.

Blue Moon

A Blue Moon occurs on the following occasions:

1 If there are two Full Moons in one calendar month, then the second is called a Blue Moon.
2 The atmosphere is polluted, and the Moon has a bluish tint or hue.

The first is considered magickal; the second means you might want to move to a new city. Use the second Full Moon in any calendar month to set long-term goals, dream big dreams, and make exciting changes—have that new makeover, change a habit, or plan a big event for yourself. A Blue Moon usually happens only every three years or so—hence the expression "once in a blue Moon."

Eclipses

No, this isn't caused by a dragon eating the Sun, as some people thought thousands of years ago. A solar eclipse happens during a New Moon, when the Moon passes directly between the Earth and the Sun, wholly or partially blocking out the Sun. A lunar eclipse happens when the Moon darkens as it passes into the Earth's shadow. (Remember: never stare at the Sun or you could damage your sight.)

Scientifically, there are three kinds of eclipses: Partial, Total, and Annular. It depends on where you live as to whether you will see them or not. Only those who are directly in the path of an eclipse can see it. We do not experience an eclipse every month because of the tilt of the Earth. On average, there are

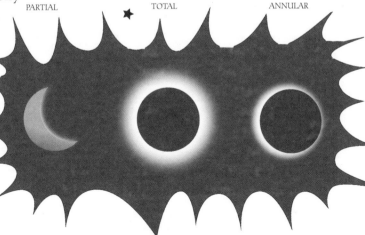

PARTIAL   TOTAL   ANNULAR

approximately five solar eclipses and two or three lunar eclipses each year.

Many magickal people believe that an eclipse signals a change and can act as a turning point in our lives. It is thought that a solar eclipse works more on an external event scale and the lunar eclipse affects us in a more personal way, coloring our emotions and changing that which is inside of us. The

trick to working with an eclipse is to:

★ Plan ahead of time precisely what you want to change in your life.

★ Begin the magickal working ten minutes before the actual eclipse occurs, and continue to work through the eclipse until you are finished. The key is to capture the energy of the eclipse and draw that energy into your working as the eclipse builds.

Thunder water

Some Witches eagerly wait for a lunar eclipse so that they can make "Thunder Water"—a kind of high-octane holy water that can banish anything negative in a very big way.

You will need:
* An almanac (so you can tell the precise time of the eclipse)
* ¼ teaspoon salt
* A small bottle of spring water (you can get this at the grocery store in pint bottles)
* A small hand mirror

Granted, you have to be able to see the eclipse to do this spell. Ten minutes before the eclipse, set up your supplies (outside is best) where you can see the Moon. Five minutes before the actual eclipse, begin chanting (or whispering) a string of words that you have made up. For example:

"Moon, magick, power, protection."

Keep repeating the words. Add three pinches of salt to the bottle. Envision the bottle glowing with its own inner blue-white light. As the Moon darkens, hold the mirror so that it catches the Moon's reflection and is positioned tilted toward the water. This may take some adjustments, so be sure to give yourself plenty of time.

Focus on the water as the eclipse occurs, continuing to say your private magickal words.
Continue to chant for at least five minutes.
When you feel you are finished, say:

"Lord and Lady, bless this water. So mote it be."

Cap the bottle and store the water in a safe place. Thunder water can be used to sprinkle around the door of your house to keep negativity from coming in, or to sprinkle on things that you don't want to throw away but that were given to you by a person you don't like (to remove their negative energy). Oh, and to throw in the face of passing vampires (just kidding!).

What if the Moon isn't in the right phase?

A young lady in her late teens once said to me, "I understand the quarters/phases of the Moon and magickal timing, but what if nothing is right but I still need to do magick? What should I do? What if I just want to take a spiritual bath or empower my jewelry before I go out on a date? Does magickal timing really matter?"

I thought very carefully for a moment or two and then I said to the girl, "It's like Raymond Buckland says. Either you want economy magick or the Ritz. With small things like empowering an item or taking a spiritual bath, you can work safely without too much preplanning. For example, you can use the magickal correspondences associated with the days of the week (see pages 84–114) or you can calculate the planetary hour.

"I remember reading somewhere that a famous Witch used to say, 'And may all astrological correspondences be correct for this working' at the end of her spells—to ensure that she got the right timing mechanism.

"Finally, no matter what, once you've been working at your magick for a while, you'll notice that your fingers will tingle when it's the right time for you to do magick, or you will have a powerful inner, driving need to perform that magick. Learn to rely on your intuition when you can't preplan or don't have much time to work out correspondences for magick."

I think that these suggestions helped the girl, and I hope that they will help you, too.

Ritual

Remember when you do magick that any ritual can be as complicated or as simple as you desire. The primary purpose of ritual is to give you a sense of fulfillment, to allow your spirit to connect in love and trust with the universe. Whether you use many Witchie tools or only your hands, the most important aspect of any ritual is how you feel. Is it any wonder, then, that since the Moon is associated with emotions, and rituals are performed to be emotionally satisfying, that these two energies work so well together?

Drawing down the Moon

We've already talked about the traditional Wiccan practice of drawing the Moon's energies into your own being. Witches do this with a variety of tools, including their hands. For the following example, we're going to draw down the Moon using your favorite flower, though you can use your hands or a mirror, if you like.

If you can, take your altar outside and find a quiet place to set up your things. Cast your magick circle, call the quarters, and speak quietly to Divinity from your heart while looking at the Moon. Anoint your forehead with oil.

Now stand facing the Moon (or in your bedroom where you can see the Moon through the window). Take a deep breath in and let it out slowly. Think first about what you want to do. Are you connecting to the Moon in the form of honoring Spirit? Are you choosing to open yourself to the gentle energy and power of the Moon? Do you have one special wish in particular that you would like granted?

Now, keeping your eyes on the Moon, slowly raise the flower with both hands and point the flower directly at the face of the Full Moon. Close your eyes for a brief moment and take another deep breath, letting it out slowly. Feel the gentle touch of the Lady as she sends her sparkling moonbeams to caress your face. Open your heart up to the positive forces of the universe, and let yourself become one with All That Is.

As you open up your inner self, you may feel a tingling, or a warm sensation, or you might feel like you are encompassed by pure love. That is the power and the glory of our Mother. If you don't, then it will come in time. When you feel you are ready, make a positive wish, directed at the Moon. Thank Deity, close the quarters, release your circle, and then quietly pack up your altar.

Moon rituals and spells

Simple Full Moon ritual in sacred space

You will need:

* The kit altar
* A real or pretend white candle
* Some incense
* Some oil for anointing
* A small piece of white paper to write your wish on
* The magickal pouch

This ritual is best done outside, but if not, try to set up your altar so that you can see the Full Moon through a window. Place the unlit candle on your altar (**never have a lit candle on your paper altar**).

Light the incense (keeping it to one side of the altar), asking Spirit to cleanse and consecrate the area. Put a small dot of anointing oil on your forehead and say:

"May I be cleansed, consecrated, and blessed in the name of Spirit. So mote it be."

Sit quietly and watch the Moon. This is such a wonderful experience, so take your time and enjoy the sounds of nature (especially if you are outside) and your view of the Moon.

When you are ready, visualize yourself surrounded by white light, then look up at the Moon, and say:

"The Moon, the light, the Witch, the love."

Repeat this at least nine times. Allow your tensions, fears, and worries to slip away from you.

If you like, draw down the Moon as I explained previously. If not, go on to the next step by holding your wish paper in your hands and thinking about how you will feel once your wish is granted. Then place the paper on your altar under the unlit candle. In your own words, tell Spirit why you need your wish granted.

Pick up the candle, think about your wish, and say:

"The Fire, the candle, the Witch, and the flame," seven times.

If you are allowed to, pick up the candle and light it (it must be in a secure holder). Repeat the chant for as long as you can, holding the candle and thinking of your wish. When you feel that you are finished, put the candle beside your altar (not too close) and allow it to burn for several minutes. If you aren't using a candle of any kind, just continue to hold your wish paper and say the chant for as long as you can.

When you are ready to pack up, thank Spirit for granting your request. You can put the candle out and then re-light it inside the house, in your room, or you can re-light the candle for five minutes every day, repeating the chant, until the candle has burned itself out. Keep your wish in your magickal charm pouch until it comes true. Then you can simply tear the paper up into tiny pieces and scatter it in the wind.

No magickal answers

Naturally, not all wishes can be granted, nor problems solved, by the use of WitchCraft. The Craft, after all, is a psychological tool to help you deal with the ups and downs of life. It is a religion. You must still make wise choices, consider all factors in any issue, and plan things with the wisdom Spirit gave you.

Sad but true, unfortunate things sometimes happen for a reason, even though we might not understand the issues right away—or ever. What is important is how we deal with the challenges and obstacles presented to us. When we work in ritual, especially with the Moon in timing, we open ourselves to our own intuition and higher selves. We allow the mystery of the universe to fill us with possibilities, with dreams, and with visions. Witches reach out to that universal knowledge to help themselves and help others. We took that oath when we started, and it is the promise we will keep to the end.

New Moon spells

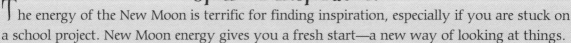

Spell for Inspiration

The energy of the New Moon is terrific for finding inspiration, especially if you are stuck on a school project. New Moon energy gives you a fresh start—a new way of looking at things.

You will need:

* Watercolor paints
(finger paints are fine for this spell)
* A watercolor brush
* Water
* Paper

For this spell, we are going to use the image of the sacred spiral (see page 45).

Sit at your desk or the kitchen table and close your eyes. Hold your hands over your supplies (paints and so on) and ask Spirit to bless them for inspiration and creativity. Using any colors, paint the sacred spiral on your paper. Your image can be as large or as small as you like; and don't worry—the design doesn't have to be perfect.

After the painted spiral is dry, ask Spirit to open your mind and allow inspiration to come to you. Trace your finger from the outside of the spiral in, thinking of positive energy moving from the outside of yourself into the creative part of yourself. You are the center of the spiral. Then trace the spiral back out again, thinking of yourself taking that inspiration and creativity, making something out of its energy and giving inspiration to the universe.

Putting problems aside

Keep doing this exercise until you get bored. When your mind wanders, it is time to stop. Don't think too hard about what you will create. Concentrate on the design and the movement of your finger. Often, when we put problems to one side for a while, solutions slide effortlessly into our brains.

Be patient. Inspiration might not come immediately, but very shortly your mind will open and you will discover just how marvelous your creativity can be! Once you have found your answer or completed your project, you can save the picture for another day, or you can dispose of it and make a new one the next time you need a little help from the muses of the universe.

Spell for true love

True love isn't necessarily finding a boyfriend or girlfriend, but you can certainly have some form of true love in your life if you try to be a good person, treat people well, and focus on universal harmony. This spell is very simple—and very helpful.

You will need:

* The kit altar
* One purple candle and stable candle holder
* A sharp pencil or needle
* Some oil—preferably sandalwood
* One rose petal (any color)
* The Earth crystal
* The silver bell
* The Magickal pouch

Next time the Moon is Full, place your altar where it will receive the Moon's empowering light. Then at New Moon, with the pencil or needle, carve your name on the candle. Rub a drop of oil into your carved name and a drop on the rose petal, focusing on drawing universal harmony into your life. Place the candle in a safe holder beside your altar. Put the rose petal in front of the candle. Hold the Earth crystal in both hands. Focus on drawing love into your life, then put the crystal on to the rose petal.

When you feel you are ready to begin, ring your silver bell four times—to summon the energies of Earth, Air, Fire, and Water. Light the wick, saying:

"Holy Mother, Moon above,
Bring to me my own true love."

Repeat this little charm nine times.

Now ring the silver bell three times, and say:

"This spell is sealed.
The love is real.
Honor is the law,
Love is the bond.
So mote it be."

Allow the candle to burn completely. Put the cold candle end, the Earth crystal, and the rose petal into the magickal pouch provided in this kit. Carry it with you to increase the love in your life. Renew on the following New Moon.

Spell for choosing the right course of study

While you are young, one of the most-asked questions to come from adults is, "And what do you want to be when you grow up?" As we barrel into our teen years, this line of questioning becomes more insistent. The school wants to know, Mom and Dad want to know, even your grandparents bug you about it. Some of your friends have their lives mapped out like a Rand McNally atlas.

If this helps, I had no clue that I was going to write books for a living until I was in my thirties! Hey, some of us take awhile, ya know? Here is a little advice I've given to my own children:

✯ Exercise your talents.
✯ Choose what you like to do best.
✯ It's okay to change your mind.

Now, you might say, "But I can't make a career out of riding my bicycle." Actually—yes, you can. You can race, or design bikes, or design bike tracks, or create a cycling video game. If you like to shop, perhaps you could be a buyer for a major company, work with the stock market, or write a book on how to find the best bargains. There is no limit to your talent or your potential. There's only the limitations you put on yourself.

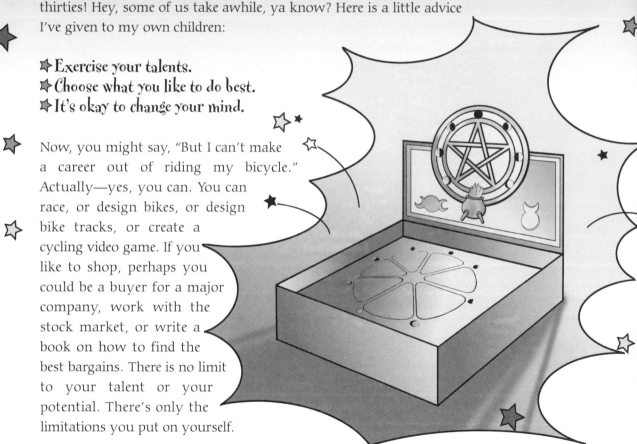

List your talents

Begin this spell by writing down all of your talents. Yes, all of them. Okay, you might want to leave out the fact that you can burp louder than anybody, but really dig deep down in yourself. Carry your list with you for one week. Read newspapers and magazines, surf the internet. Suppose you thought, "Gee, I wonder what it would be like to be a judge?" Don't wonder any longer! Go visit a courtroom. "What's it like to be an artist?" Ask one.

At the end of the week, place your list of talents on your kit altar, hold your hands over the list, and say:

"Within each person lies many talents, a potential beyond their wildest dreams. I ask that Spirit help me to recognize my potential and my talents. Please bring to me the opportunity to learn more about myself in a positive way, so that I may choose the right course of study for me. Please open the doors to the destiny that is right for me, and close the doors tight on those paths that would lead me astray. As I will, so mote it be!"

Ring your kit's silver bell four times—one ring to bring aid from each of the elemental compass points.

Keep your list of talents with you until you have chosen a course of study. Before you make your final decision, read the list one more time. If you feel that you are not being true to yourself, reading the list will give you the opportunity to change your mind.

Spell for sending a friend off with love
(This spell can also be done the day before your friend leaves.)

Sometimes, either you or a friend must move away. When Witches move out of traveling distance from one another, they often hold a parting ceremony at the New (or the Full) Moon. All of the coven gathers, and a ceremony is performed in order to bestow on the individual who is leaving the blessings of love and safe travel. Gifts are also given, and the ceremony is completed with a wonderful feast.

If you have a friend who is leaving, and you wish to have a ceremony of your own (and they are willing to take part), you, too, can exchange gifts—such as a bracelet, key chain, or other memento. You might also like to perform the following ceremony, written by David Norris of the Black Forest Tradition just for you. Say these words:

> *"Gently as we bid farewell*
> *Oh how I hate to see you go*
> *Only Spirit understands the*
> *Deep regret that we will know*
> *But we will never truly part*
> *You will always be with me*
> *Ever in my mind and heart*
> *Goodbye, for now, farewell to thee."*

Now perform this touching ceremony:

You will need:

* Two white candles and holders
* Something you can place underneath the candles to catch wax drips
* Silver, gold, or yellow cord (not the kit one, as you give it to your friend at the end)

Find a place where the two of you can be alone. Place the candles in holders in the middle of the floor on a table where you will be sitting. If you aren't allowed candles, then omit this part, or perhaps your parents would like to join in—how lovely to perform this ceremony together with two complete families! Hold each other's hands and cast a circle in your mind or out loud—whatever you prefer. Once you are enclosed in the circle, sit down across from each other and light the candles. Say the following words:

> *"This is the light of our friendship that will never go out."*

Once you light the candles and the flame is burning brightly, each person picks up the cord in turn. One at a time, tell each other of the good times you have had together, marking each reminiscence by tying a knot in the cord. Every time you tell your friend something that you really like about them, tie another knot. If you talk about some difficulty that you helped each other through, tie a knot of remembrance. If there is something funny that you both did, or that happened to you, tie a knot as you laugh about it. There will be a few tears mixed in with the laughter, but they are tears of love, so do not be concerned. You might want to do all of this by simply passing the cord back and forth between the two of you.

Continue telling these stories for as long as you want to. You'll probably end up tying the cord full of knots. When you've finished, place the cord between you and say together, or in turn:

"These are our memories, take them with you."

Sit quietly for a moment and consider how much you have been blessed to be friends. Now, take the candles and tip both forward slightly until the flames touch briefly. Then say in unison:

"Two flames, one light of friendship that never goes out."

Extinguish the candles and swap the one you have held with your friend. When you are ready, hold hands again and open the circle, which has enclosed you. When that is done, say together:

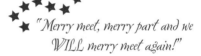

"Merry meet, merry part and we WILL merry meet again!"

Soon the time will come when you will really have to say goodbye. But when that time comes, you will be able to remember those good times you talked about in your magick circle. And if you feel particularly lonely, you can light the friendship candle you were given and remember the light of that friendship.

Some friends find that, even though they are apart, if they think about each other, one or the other will end up calling on the phone, or a letter or e-mail will arrive. After all, friendship is the truest magick of all.

Spell to find direction in life and stop drifting

Sometimes we feel as if we are drifting on an open sea without direction. When there are so many ways that we can navigate through life that it can be difficult to choose which way you should go, try this spell.

You will need:

✦ A white candle (or flashlight or whatever)
✦ A large bowl of water
✦ A small plastic boat (the type you can get inexpensively at a store— or you can make one yourself)

Be tolerant

Something you should always consider when doing ritual work while you are living with guardians is this: always abide by the wishes of those people who provide a home for you. Yes, that means being honorable about complying with their requests. If they have asked you not to burn candles, for example, you should do what they ask. You may not understand a request, it may not even seem reasonable, but honor is the law of our Craft, and you should do what they have asked simply because it is the right thing to do.

In the case of candles, there are many ways to get along without them, as I said before. Wiccans believe that there is both a physical fire and a spiritual fire. So use imaginary candles and symbolically light them, as I suggested a little while back. In the spell for parting, a good alternative is to turn on two flashlights instead of lighting candles, and then let the beams shine together before turning them out. Give each other the flashlight you have held—for keeps—and that will be the light of friendship that each can turn on when you think of each other.

Take your lit white candle, pretend candle, or flashlight and place it beside the bowl of water. Place your little boat in the bowl of water. Relax and watch the boat float. If you've made the boat yourself, perhaps you painted your name on it. Imagine that you are on this boat.

Out on the water

Sit quietly and try this visualization exercise. Imagine yourself out on the open water in this boat. Make the boat anything you wish it to be, a sailboat, a motor boat, a yacht, a cruiser—anything that you are in control of. You are at the wheel. If you feel that your life or decisions are aimless, the waters might be a little choppy in your visualization.

Begin to see/feel the waters around you getting calmer and settling down until they are only gentle waves or as still as glass. Once you have done that, look off to the horizon and visualize land. The land represents your goal. This doesn't have to be anything very specific, just a state of happiness and a place where you want to be. See yourself slowly turning the boat toward that shore. Say nine times:

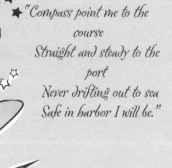

"Compass point me to the course
Straight and steady to the port
Never drifting out to sea
Safe in harbor I will be."

Closer and closer you'll get until you can see everything on land. Maybe you'll even see some of your friends waving to you as you move near to the dock. When you think you are close enough (or you feel yourself losing the picture/feeling in your mind), imagine a line reaching out and being tied to the first post at the dock. You are being safely pulled in, and you cannot drift away. See yourself being pulled into shore and lines being tied to the bow and stern of the boat. Visualize as many lines holding you to shore as you think you need. Begin to say to yourself:

"Lines to Earth
Lines to shore
Lines to hold fast evermore
Lines of safety
Lines of peace
Lines to make my drifting cease."

Visualization

Don't worry if you have a hard time actually "seeing" yourself in your mind in the boat or on the water. Just concentrate on thinking about how you would feel. Pictures aren't necessary. Visualization takes practice.

Say this over and over as many times as you feel comfortable. When you feel balanced and under control, relax—you are there! Take the boat out of the water, let it dry and put it in a special place. Any time you feel you are drifting through life, take out the boat and repeat the spell. Soon, you will be able to visualize a specific destination for your boat. When that happens, repeat the spell, giving a name to the dock where you will finish your visualization.

Spell for spirituality

Spirituality isn't a particular religion—it is your personal interaction with God/dess. This spell connects you with spirituality and will also empower the silver moon pendant provided in your kit.

First, make some holy water (see page 53) and then set it aside in a bowl. During the New Moon, place your kit altar on a table or dresser. If you like, light two white candles for illumination. Place a dot of oil (preferably sandalwood) on your forehead and say:

You will need:
* Holy water
* A bowl
* The kit altar
* Two white candles or equivalents
* Oil for anointing
* Some incense
* The silver moon pendant
* A red candle or similar
* Some salt

"Blessed are my feet that walk in the light of the Lord and Lady.
Blessed are my knees that kneel at the sacred altar.
Blessed is my heart that beats pure and true.
Blessed are my lips that utter the words of truth and wisdom.
Blessed are my eyes so that they may see within and without.
Blessed is my mind that does not judge lest I be judged.
Blessed is my spirit that seeks to unite with Divinity.
So mote it be."

Light some incense and pass your pendant through the smoke of the incense, saying:

"This pentacle is cleansed and consecrated in the name of the Lord and Lady. Gifts from the spirits of Air within you. So mote it be."

Now light a red votive candle and pass the pendant through the flame, saying:

"This pentacle is cleansed and consecrated in the name of the Lord and Lady. Gifts from the spirits of Fire within you. So mote it be."

Sprinkle the holy water on the pendant and say:

"This pentacle is cleansed and consecrated in the name of the Lord and Lady. Gifts of the spirits of Water within you. So mote it be."

Sprinkle a little salt on the pendant and say:

"This pentacle is cleansed and consecrated in the name of the Lord and Lady. Gifts of the spirits of Earth within you. So mote it be."

Make an equal-armed cross on the back of the pendant with a dot of the sandalwood oil, saying:

"This pentacle is cleansed and consecrated in the name of the Lord and Lady. I call down the power of the Holy Mother and Father to surround this pentacle for protection, love, and harmony. So mote it be!"

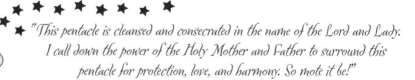

Envision white light surrounding the pendant. It may grow hot or vibrate in your hand. This is normal. Your silver moon pentacle pendant is now ready to wear! Cleanse it each year on your birthday.

Spells for the time between New Moon and First Quarter (Half Moon)

Most of us love to shop—right? Over the next few pages you'll find some great shopping spells. Hold the prosperity coin in your hand as you do magick, and you'll get even better bargains. Between New Moon and First Quarter is the ideal time to window shop for things you want to buy in the future (but not right now).

Spell for successful window shopping

I tried magick using a finger puppet when I was eleven years old, and it worked pretty well—try it for yourself! Make yourself a finger puppet, hold it in your hands and repeat what it is you want over and over. Your puppet is now empowered to help you find great deals that you can go back to later, when the Moon is in the First Quarter. Carry the puppet in your pocket. Don't tell anyone, though—magick shared is magick lost.

Spells for the time from the First Quarter to the day before the Full Moon

It's okay to get the big stuff now, like that expensive dress you've been dying to wear to the dance (it may even be on sale), or those CDs you've been saving your pennies for.

Spell for shopping guidance

Did anyone ever say to you, "Money doesn't grow on trees"? Well, trees can be extremely magickal and helpful. Every tree has a specific association. For example, while maple trees are associated with prosperity, oaks stand for strength. However, if you are nice to them, most trees will assist you on any issue. When I was very young, I created what I called my own "soul magick" as I went along. If you twirl a tree leaf by the stem, you can create magick through the repetition of motion and the focus of your mind. That's all you have to do with this spell.

So, find a leaf, sit quietly, and concentrate on bringing the best buys possible toward you as you roll the stem in your hands. Take the leaf with you while you shop. I bet you'll be amazed at your success! (If you must pluck a leaf, rather than finding one on the ground, don't forget to ask the tree for permission first.)

Spells for the day before and the day of the Full Moon

Now, on the day before, and the day of, the Full Moon you'll find that impulse buying will strike like lightning, sucking your hard-earned cash from your wallet faster than Dorothy flew to Oz. In fact, don't take your purse with you if you plan to go to the mall, and for pity's sake, stay away from any credit cards!

Spell to keep me from shopping

If temptation does strike, try this spell I learned from my grandmother. Before you go to a store, literally tie your paper money, checkbook, bank card (and credit cards if you have them) with red yarn. As you wind the yarn around your spending power, say the following:

"I keep my money close to me
Far from the shores of bankrupt sea."

That's all there is to it. Keep repeating the chant, then tie off the yarn, visualizing your money staying with you. Under a different Quarter Moon, when it is time to spend that cash, slowly remove the red yarn, visualizing your freedom to spend your money on what you truly want.

References for Moon phases and shopping spells in *Moon Magic*, by Lori Reid, Crown Publishers, NY, NY, 1998.

Spells for the Full Moon

Spell to find a lost object

How many times have you ripped your room apart trying to find something at the last minute? In the magick circle, the North is the place of manifestation. This compass point is where energy from the universe joins with that of the Earth plane. In ritual, your circle is a barrier, allowing only the energies you specify to come inside. If you wish to manifest something on the Earth plane, use the vortex of the North to help you by raising the right kind of energy inside the circle.

Sometimes though, when we lose something and we're in a hurry, there isn't any time to cast a magick circle, call the North quarter, and then voice our request. So here's a little spell to help you when time is of the essence and you've got to find your homework before the bus (or your ride) takes you to school.

Stand facing North. Take a deep breath and imagine that you are one with the universe. Hold your right hand in the air, a little above your head with your palm up. Visualize in your mind exactly what you lost. If you can't visualize very well, imagine how you will feel when you find the object. Keeping the picture or feeling in your mind, say in an authoritative way:

*"Wolves and fairies, dragons and ghosts
I've lost the thing that I need most.
My [whatever you lost] is gone, it must be found
Whether lost above or below the ground.
Bring it back as quick as can be
As I will, so mote it be!"*

Keep looking for the lost object, allowing your intuition to guide you. Above all, don't panic or get frustrated. If, after a few minutes of looking, you haven't found the lost object, repeat the spell. Each object you own does carry your signature energy and can find its way home if the universe is in agreement. If the object doesn't turn up quickly, practice this spell every morning or evening for seven days. If you haven't found your possession after seven days, it may well be that it decided to take a vacation or find a new owner. Hey, it happens. Remember this: Things are just things, after all.

Spell for getting along with siblings

It isn't always easy to get along with our sister(s) or brother(s). Sometimes they are simply a major pain, but you know that the family environment is important, which probably stresses you out when you lose your temper. Try this simple little spell.

You will need:

* Some paper (newsprint will do)
* A pair of scissors
* A black marker pen
* Some glue
* The silver bell
* A rubber band
* A large bowl of sugar

Cut out rough paper shapes to represent the people in your family involved in specific problems or clashes. On each paper person, write the name of a family member associated with that figure. Be sure to make a little person for yourself, too! When you are finished, glue the dolls together, saying:

*"Love and understanding surrounds us
Moves through us
Becomes us."*

Repeat the charm nine times, then ring your silver bell three times, saying:

*"As I will, it now is done,
From the blushing of the dawn
To the setting of the Sun,
From the rise of the Moon
Until it slips from morning light,
The love we need will surround us,
Never out of sight."*

Now roll up your paper people, wrap the rubber band around them, and place deep in the sugar bowl. (Make sure that the glue is dry first, though!)

Spell to cope with peer pressure

No matter how old you are, one of the hardest challenges any of us must overcome is dealing with negative peer pressure. If you are having such a problem, remember that it is okay to talk to a guardian—they love you and will try to give you the best advice they can. Then, at the beginning of the Full Moon and every morning thereafter, hold the golden prosperity coin from the kit in your hand and say:

*"Mother of Wisdom, Father of Courage
Make the pathway I am walking
Free of friendship's bright temptations.
Let me say words I would say.
Let me do things I would do.
Let me honor who I am
As much as my friends desire.
Let me clearly see the choices
That I must make every day.
Let me build on every minute.
Let me be strong every hour.
Let me do the things I choose,
And not cause harm,
Even to me."*

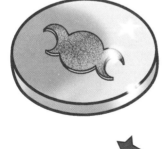
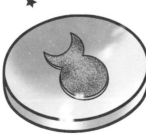

Spell to prepare for the future

You will need:

* A pack of small index cards or slips of paper of equal size
* A blue or purple pen (both are spiritual colors)
* Your hopes and dreams!
* A paper punch
* Some purple ribbon

Although we can't know precisely what the future holds, Spirit has given us an element of control—our minds. We may have to work really hard at our goals, but we have the power to get there. To prepare for the future, you must have a plan. Using story boards, as they do in cartoons and film, can be a nifty planning technique. Try it!

On a Full Moon, take the cards outside (or near a window where the light of the Moon peeks in the room) and hold them in the moonlight. Ask Spirit to help you plan for your future. You may want to use one of the grounding or centering exercises in the book to help you, or you may wish to draw down the Moon. After some hard thinking, write down on the cards what you truly want in life. Take as long as you like. Dream big! When you are finished, hold the cards under the moonlight again, and say: ✦

✦ *"Great Mother, I hold my future in my hands. These are my hopes and dreams. I realize that, as I grow older, my choices may change, but for now these are the things I most ardently desire."*

Hold the cards out, as if you are offering them to Spirit, and say: ✦

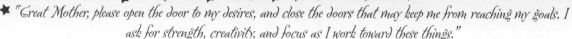

✦ *"Great Mother, please open the door to my desires, and close the doors that may keep me from reaching my goals. I ask for strength, creativity, and focus as I work toward these things."*

Say aloud the things you wish to manifest, followed by this chant: ✦

✦ *"Earth and Fire, Water will flow,
Air to make the magick go."*

Repeat the chant nine times. Punch a hole in each card and thread ribbon through. In the morning, take your cards outside and hang them in a tree or a bush. You could decorate them with glitter or drawings. If you don't want anyone to read the words, just use pictures, but you must write down somewhere (perhaps in a journal) precisely what it is that you desire for your future. You need to make the thought whole.

Start now!

As time passes, you should actively work toward your goals. For example, if you want to become an artist, then study the masters of the past and put paints to paper (or canvas) yourself. Don't stress over it, just look upon it as trying on your future for size.

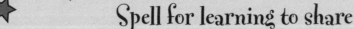

Spell for learning to share

This can be a tough one! Sharing anything can be hard. We don't want to get nasty over it, but this often happens when we feel that we don't have enough of the limelight. Although we can learn by example how to share, it's up to each of us to incorporate that sharing attitude in our lives. Sharing actually makes you feel better—all warm and fuzzy inside, especially if it has made another person happy. When times are hard financially, we tend to grasp at things a little harder.

Next time you have a "non-sharing" moment, try holding your magickal pentacle in the palm of your hand while repeating this little spell:

"Goddess, help me,
I don't know what to do.
I want [say whatever it is]
But he/she wants it, too.
Goddess, help me,
I wish to do what's right
But part of me is not so sure,
And so I've got a fight.
Goddess, please help me
To understand their view.
Teach me to share,
To do what's right and true.
Goddess, thank you,
For showing me the way.
With love and light and happiness,
I'll learn to share this day."

Spell to help a friend who's down

This is a wonderful spell for a friend or family member going through a bad patch, especially if they mention they've been having trouble sleeping at night. Physical exercise, eating properly, and daily meditations can also help, as can being creative—drawing, painting, singing, playing music, writing poetry, or short stories, etc. If the condition becomes chronic, though, they should take a trip to the doctor.

You will need:

* Some paper and a pen
* A small purple bag
* A teaspoon of crushed lavender
* A bit of crushed rosemary
* Some ribbon or needle and thread (purple, preferably)
* A dab of your favorite oil or perfume

The Black Swan

The Black Swan of DreamTime is an old legend of the Australian aboriginal people, who believe that the Black Swan carries us into a safe and loving place of dreaming.

Write the name of the person you want to help (this might be yourself) on a slip of paper. Fill the bag with the herbs and add the paper slip. Tie or sew the open end of the bag shut. Put a drop of the oil or perfume on the bag. Crush the bag in both hands, and say:

"Black Swan, take me on your dark wings
Gliding through your dream-veiled door
Across the blackened pond of sleep
Past shadows to the DreamTime shore.

"Safely sleeping as I travel
Over waters of the mind
And in the magick of my dreaming
I leave my problems far behind.

"Black Swan, guide me as I'm waking
Carry me in comfort home
And when I wake reveal the mystery
Then every answer will be known."

David O. Norris

Place the dream sachet under your/your friend's pillow to enjoy a pleasant night's sleep! Renew every thirty days. You can use the bag contained in your kit if sleep assistance is temporary.

Spells for the day after the Full Moon until the Last Quarter

Back to shopping again. This is value time—more power in your purse. Look for the sales and you'll find them. Amaze your friends as you lead them to the best buys (which, of course, you carefully observed when the Moon was in her First Quarter). No specific spell here—perhaps you can try creating one of your own! And don't forget the Good Deals Spell (below).

Spell to guide me to good deals

You will need:

✤ A little fresh mint, which you can buy in the produce section at the grocery store
✤ A wooden box
✤ A little honey
✤ A little planning on your part!

The day after the Full Moon, crush the mint and place it in the box. Wipe a little honey on the inside lid of the box. Think of the honey attracting good deals and savings for you. Allow the box to stand open as the mint dries.

Throughout the month, every time you get a little extra change, or a wandering coin or bill or two, hold the money in your hands and envision it growing. Then say:

"You will only be able to be spent on a good deal."

Throw the money in the box. When you are ready to shop for a deal, take only a small amount of money from the box (bill or change). Leave the rest. Add the money you've taken from the box to the other money you have to spend in your purse. As you put the money in your back pocket or purse, say:

"I will be guided to great deals where I will get the best value!"

When you get home, add up how much money you saved. Put the same amount of money you took out of the box back in, and repeat the same message:

"You will only be able to be spent on a good deal."

Not only will you be training your mind to look for value, but you will also have learned how to save!

Spells for the Last Quarter to the day before the New Moon

When it comes to shopping, you might find that salespeople aren't very helpful around this time, somewhat like the Full Moon phase. Be prepared for problems—the store has that pair of shoes in every size but yours and so on. Be careful with your money, as your thinking may be foggy—forgetting your bank card, etc. Buy only what you absolutely must have and wait for a better time to make other purchases.

Spells for the Dark of the Moon

Time to take a total break from shopping. Instead, go swimming, play football, have a slumber party—time for a little fun and a rest for your savings account. Here are some non-shopping spells to perform at this time:

Spell for bringing matters to a close

Take a black shoelace or cord and tie as many knots in it as you can. Think of all the loose ends that you need to tie up. As you tie the knots, repeat the following verse:

"Endings, endings, new beginnings
Wheel of life is spinning free.
Bring this matter to conclusion
Make it final, make me free.
Ever turning, to completion
Soon its time has passed away.
Open up each bright new vista
From sunset to light of day.
Endings, endings, new beginnings,
Closing doors are wide again.
The wheel of life is ever turning
Never fear what may have been.
Frost will shroud the summer garden
Gone are flowers, season done.
Blooms may die, yet seeds are sleeping
Then reawakened by the Sun."

Now take the black cord outside and bury it off your property.

Spell for uncovering the truth

If you expect the truth, you must try your best to offer truth in return. That said, if you wish to find the truth of any matter, you can use the quartz crystal in your kit to ferret out the needed information. As a warning, prying into folks' business that does not concern you is a Witchie no-no.

Hold the quartz crystal in your hand, take a deep breath, and close your eyes. Concentrate on discovering the truth of the matter. Don't let your logical mind try to work through the scenario just yet. Be calm, relax. Hold the crystal in your hand until it feels warm, and say:

"The truth of the matter lies within the eye of the tiger. I understand and see that which is appropriate for me to know. I feel the tiger on the prowl, looking for the truth. His paws tread lightly through the forest of confusion. He knows the way. He is strong, sure, and careful. The tiger knows the path to all knowledge. I follow the tiger."

Ring your silver bell seven times, then say:

"The truth of the matter lies within the eye of the tiger. I understand and see that which is appropriate for me to know. Through the tiger, I am looking to find the truth about _____ [state your question]. His cunning guides me to the light of knowledge. He is vibrant. He is powerful and follows the beat of the drums of accuracy. He travels the pathway of truth, this crystal hung about his beautiful neck. I hear the message of the tiger."

You may have a moment of clarity immediately, or you may have to wait for the information to come to you. Put the crystal in your pocket and carry it with you until you discern the truth of the matter. Before starting, it's best to cleanse the crystal in sunlight, moonlight, or under running water.

Spell for dealing with death

Wiccan Witches believe that when a person (or a pet) passes away, they still have the ability to hear you and be with you. We believe that there is a truly wonderful place beyond our realms of understanding called the Summerland, where we go when we leave this world to recover, learn—and wait until we return once again.

Closure

When dealing with death, we need a sense of closure. It is thought that there is a resting time from death until the person is able to communicate with you. This time can be as short as a few days or may last several months. Eventually, you may have a dream that they are okay, or receive a gift that reminds you of the deceased, or suddenly think of them out of the blue. In truth, they are communicating with you.

First, light a candle (the person's favorite color) or place flowers (the kind that they liked best) on a table and lay your magickal pentacle pendant around the candle or over the flowers. Have a box of tissues ready—it is perfectly healthy to cry. Cast your magick circle and then sit in the center of it. Say the person's name three times, then read the following prayer:

"You have gone and now I wonder
Why it is you must depart.
And even though you're just a memory
Your spark of life is in my heart.
No tears or wishing bring you back,
No hope can change this plan of time.
I must wait as you go onward
Into those Summerlands divine.
The Sun in this world, where you left me,
Rises, shining, then descends,
Setting in the western quarter
Yet soon to come back up again.
Within your land there is no shadow
And love eternal never dies.
I know you're with me every moment
Even through this brief goodbye."

This moving prayer was written by David O. Norris. It should, hopefully, help you to get through the separation that we perceive is caused by death.

If you can, let the candle burn right down until there is nothing left. If your parents say that you aren't allowed to have candles, then perhaps they will sit with you while you light the taper and read the poem with you aloud. Death is, after all, meant to bring us all closer together.

Spell for Divine Justice

 Sometimes things just get out of hand, and events become more serious than we can imagine. Justice will correct injustice and return balance. Maybe you have been misjudged or accused of something you didn't do. Large or small, the scales of Justice are waiting to be tipped in favor of what is right. Here's what to do.

First, understand that Divine Justice is truly blind and will make corrections wherever necessary. If you don't have clean hands in the matter, then ask Spirit for forgiveness, and do whatever is needed to balance the scales yourself. If you (or the person you are working for) are guilty, you cannot expect everything to be as it was before. However, Spirit does not intend that you be punished and ruined, especially if you have learned from what you did wrong. Doing this spell will help balance the scales so that whatever happens will be in your best interest and you will be protected from overreaction by the forces against you.

Before you start, sit quietly and calm your feelings about the situation as best you can. In this spell you will be calling in the energy of Goddess Maat—the Egyptian goddess of Divine Order and Justice—to bring you justice.

Settling accounts

First settle accounts within yourself, then begin working with Maat. When you are ready, print your full name at the top of the paper. Then, without lifting the pen off the paper, draw a square around your name, making sure that all of the lines meet. While you do this, envision that a wall of protection is being placed around you. This wall will remain until the problem is resolved. Then write the name of the person who is against you, or a keyword that encompasses the situation. After you have done this, hold the paper in both hands, and say:

"I call you, Maat, I call for Justice.
Rise, come forth and bring your scales
To balance life and right injustice,
Let trouble end and truth prevail."

You will need:

* A piece of orange paper
* A black marker pen
* An envelope
* Scissors

Remain quiet for a few moments and imagine Maat's overshadowing presence coming to do the work you need. When you feel the moment is right, take the pen and write over the top of the other person's name, or keyword, the four letters "MAAT." What you are doing is covering the person or incident with the power of the Goddess of Justice. Write the letters slowly and with a clear understanding that peace, harmony, and truth will prevent the individual, or the momentum of the situation, from acting contrary to Divine Justice.

Now take the paper and fold it into three parts so that it will fit into the envelope. You fold it in three parts to represent the beginning of the problem, your understanding of the present situation, and your recognition that the problem will soon end in a just manner. Now seal it in the envelope and write on the outside of the envelope in large letters "MAAT." Place it under a light somewhere to represent the Light of Justice shining on the situation.

The next day, take your scissors and slowly cut three narrow strips off the right side of the envelope, one at a time, letting them fall in a wastebasket. While you are cutting them off, say the following words:

> *"By this act I cut injustice*
> *And let each portion fall away.*
> *Truth prevails, my future brightens*
> *Maat, bring Justice here to stay."*

Say this three times, one for each strip you cut away. When you have cut the three strips off, hold the envelope between your two palms, and say:

> *"Goddess Maat, injustice dwindles*
> *All conforming to your plan.*
> *Please return and bring your balance*
> *Justice rules the hearts of man."*

Put the remainder of the envelope away for use the next day. Empty the pieces out of your wastebasket and out of your house. Do this every day until you have cut the envelope and its contents completely into pieces and nothing remains. Then say:

*"Now the scales of life are balanced
Justice reigns in truth again.
Humbly I accept your verdict
Goddess Maat bring forth your plan.
Equal Justice, equal magick,
Let your power set me free.
Work your will, and set the record,
Justice for eternity!"*

If you feel you need to do this process again, do it two more times with two more pieces of paper and two more envelopes. This will ensure that you remain consistent with the rhythm of three that we have been using in this working. If you get Justice or receive your answer before you have cut all the remaining strips away, don't stop. Continue the spell to the very end to ensure that Divine Justice will remain.

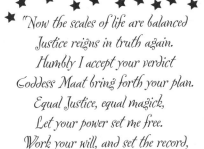

Spell for increased psychic power

*"In the stillness and the quiet
Of the flame within my soul,
Let me listen to the echoes of
That magick in its glow.
Let the voices all around me
Speak in harmony and light.
Let me yearn to hear their meaning,
Let me learn to know what's right.
When the 'still soft voice' is speaking,
Let me listen in that hour.
When my angels stand around me
Let me see their magick power.
May bright heavens' mysteries open.
May the veil be drawn away.
May I walk with guides and know them
Every moment of the day."*

Repeat this lovely prayer each evening before you go to bed.

Spells for when the Moon is Void of Course

Okay. What about shopping during this phase? Historically, an item purchased during a Void Moon will:

* Break before the warranty runs out.
* Be defective as soon as you try to use it.
* Cost you more than you bargained for.
* Lose its interest almost before you get it home.
* Be the wrong size, although you SWEAR you checked the tag.

Conclusion: do not buy anything (as if you needed telling!).

Magickal money tips

✿ When you pay for anything—no matter which phase the Moon is in—hand paper money over to the salesperson folded in half with the fold toward the other person. Open the folded bill(s) slightly as you hand it over, so that you can see the crease. As the money opens, the energy comes back to you, adding to your continued prosperity. (No, this doesn't hurt the other person's financial status.)

✿ Sprinkle your paper money with cinnamon, visualizing your money coming back to you tenfold. Brush off any excess cinnamon.

✿ Don't flash your money around when shopping, and keep how much you have with you to yourself. Some of your friends might not be as honest as you are, and some friends might try to get you to spend your money unwisely. If they don't know how much you have, then they can't suggest you purchase something that you know you can't afford or don't need.

✿ Write your own spell to match the phases of the Moon and perform that spell before you go to the mall to increase your financial wizardry.

Magickal spells for every day

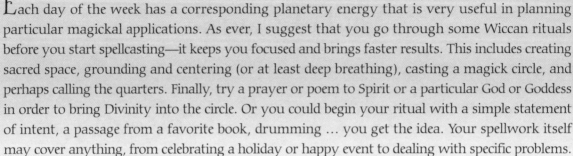

Each day of the week has a corresponding planetary energy that is very useful in planning particular magickal applications. As ever, I suggest that you go through some Wiccan rituals before you start spellcasting—it keeps you focused and brings faster results. This includes creating sacred space, grounding and centering (or at least deep breathing), casting a magick circle, and perhaps calling the quarters. Finally, try a prayer or poem to Spirit or a particular God or Goddess in order to bring Divinity into the circle. Or you could begin your ritual with a simple statement of intent, a passage from a favorite book, drumming ... you get the idea. Your spellwork itself may cover anything, from celebrating a holiday or happy event to dealing with specific problems.

How to work with the days of the week

In this magickal days section, I've listed spells under the day when you are more likely to be successful. Keep in mind that:

* ✱ If the Moon is full, there is more power on that day.
* ✱ If the Moon is new, then this day represents a "beginning time."
* ✱ If the Moon is waxing (growing larger, between the New Moon and the Full Moon), then this will be a building day.
* ✱ If waning (growing smaller, between the Full Moon and the New Moon), this will be a banishing or tying-up-loose-ends day.

All of this means you may want to reword the day spells to match the Moon phase. If this seems too hard, don't worry, just work the spells as they are. As you learn more, things will fall into place. The same goes for spells where you don't have all the ingredients and so on—you'll soon learn to use your ingenuity.

Colors for the days of the week

Each day of the week has special color associations. So, for example, if you would like to use candles in your spellwork, you might wish to begin with these color correspondences.

Monday ✱ ✱ ✱ White, Blue, or Silver
Tuesday ✱ ✱ ✱ Red or Orange
Wednesday ✱ ✱ Purple
Thursday ✱ ✱ ✱ Green
Friday ✱ ✱ ✱ ✱ Blue or Pink
Saturday ✱ ✱ ✱ Black
Sunday ✱ ✱ ✱ Yellow or Gold

Monday ~ Moon day spells

On Monday, work magick related to these issues:

Children, parents, family issues, pregnancy, female health issues, pets, real estate, emotions, intuition, visionary work, dreams, the element of Water, boating, swimming, and temporary plans. All of these have strong links to feminine Moon energies. On Mondays, read about dreams, divination, etc., to develop psychic abilities. Focus on which emotions belong to you and which may belong to others (but you were internalizing these and didn't even know it!).

Make your own magick mirror

Making your own magick mirror—always on a Monday—helps you to get in touch with your inner self.

You will need:

✿ Some light—a candle, desk lamp, or the light of the Full Moon … whatever

✿ Black ink

✿ A small bowl filled with water

✿ Paper and pen

Work by the light of the Moon or a lamp. Hold your hands over the ink and ask that Spirit (or your favorite divinity) bless it. Do the same thing with the water. Pour the ink carefully into the water (black ink can stain horribly). Make a list of the things you would like to think about, or a single solution that you may need. Draw a symbol of the Moon on the paper. Place the list under the bowl.

Close your eyes and relax. Ground, center, and cast a circle. Take a deep breath, relax, and then look into the bowl of black water—no, you won't see anything scary there. Now, ask Spirit for a solution to your problem or question. Think of your mind reaching out, touching Spirit, and coming back with the answer. Be patient, breathe deeply, and focus your mind.

When an answer has come to you, or you feel that you are finished, thank your deity, remove your circle, and dispose of the water. Tear up the paper with your list, thinking about how you will feel when the problem is solved, and throw the pieces away. Don't worry if the solution didn't come to you right on the spot. It may take a few days for your mind to sort through the problem. You may receive an answer in a dream or from a friend. Leave the possibilities open!

Spells for moving into a new house

Moving from one home to another is a shock to the system. It's hard to reorient yourself, make new friends, and discover which areas of the new town or city are safe. Houses, like people, have a personality of their own. They collect energy just like any other inanimate object. A place that is new to you should be thoroughly cleaned, and then blessed, in order to fill it with harmonious energies.

First spell ~ spell to bless this house

When you move into your new home, begin by finding a place to put your kit altar. Lay a representation of each element (Earth, Air, Fire, and Water) around it. Take a deep breath, then ground and center. Carry the four elements around your home (not forgetting any attics and basements, front and back yards, sheds, garages, etc.).

Once you are finished, stand in each room/area and ask Divinity to enter the area and bless your home. Finally, seal each window and door by sprinkling crushed cloves (or making the sign of a pentacle with your index finger) by all openings. Then stand in the center of your home and ring your kit silver bell seven times, asking Divinity to enter your home and bless all who live there.

Once a month, mix a teaspoon of fresh orange juice with a gallon of water and sprinkle it around your home to keep it fresh. Pay close attention to doors and windows. If you feel afraid at any time, seal the openings with your finger by drawing a pentacle in the air over the door or window. If there is anger or frustration in the home, mix a little basil (from the grocery store) with a teaspoon of lemon juice. Pour the mixture into a bottle of spring water. Shake vigorously, then sprinkle it all around the house. Pay special attention to rooms where the most negativity appears to collect.

Naturally, sprinkling a little water won't stop something as serious as an abusive guardian or those who are hooked on drugs. For serious problems, check out the help information (page 122).

Second spell ~ spell to forge new friendships

Once you have moved into your new home, it's time to look for some good new friends. Write down the qualities you seek in a friend on a piece of paper. Place it in a small plastic bag with a cup of brown sugar. Hold the bag, close your eyes, and ask Spirit to help you choose wisely and bring you a true friend. Place the bag in a safe place until the friendships manifest, then sprinkle the sugar outside the house, asking for continued harmony in your life. Then burn the paper or tear it into small pieces.

Spell to bring food into the home

Even in rich countries, thousands of children and adults go hungry every day. If there isn't enough food to eat, swallow your pride and ask for help from someone you trust. They might be able to tell you about associations that help with this kind of problem.

You will need:

* A bag of popping corn (the microwave kind is easiest)
* A piece of thread

If you have to pop popcorn the old-fashioned way and you're not allowed to use the stove, have an adult help you.

If you have a microwave, all the better, but be careful when you open the hot bag. Either way, hold your hands over the unpopped kernels and ask Spirit to increase the volume of good food in your home as the heat expands the popcorn. As the kernels begin to pop, think of the negativity in the house exploding and an unlimited abundance of food coming into the home. String a handful of the popcorn on a piece of thread and hang it on the refrigerator door. As you hang the string, ask Spirit to bring you the food that you need.

Spell to help your parents or guardian

The spell here is simply to give them a treat or a hug or be especially helpful. Being nice to others is a pretty magickal thing to do— Witches take an Oath of Service that they will help humanity.

Spells for healing a friend, relative, or pet

Always encourage sick people to visit a doctor—magick and science work best when used together. Sickness can be scary, but remember that spells and prayers are the same . Nothing you can do will make matters worse. Do all that is in your power, and that's the best you can do.

First spell ~ the healing picture spell

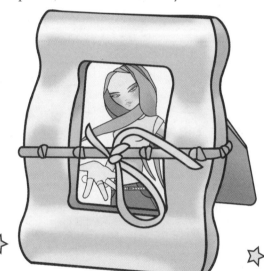

You will need:
* A photo of, or item belonging to, the sick person
* Golden wish cord

Healing magick works best when you have something belonging to the sick person to work with—Witches call this working "in sympathy." For this spell, hold your golden wish cord over the picture/item and say:

"With knot of one, my spell's begun." Tie a loose knot at one end of the cord.

"With knot of two, my word is true." Tie a second knot close to the first.

"With knot of three, I bring healing to thee." Tie the third knot. Say the patient's full name three times.

"By knot of four, you're better than before." Tie the fourth knot.

"By knot of five, this spell's alive." Tie the fifth knot.

"By knot of six, you are no longer sick!" Tie the sixth knot.

"Seventh knot sealed, you are healed!" Tie the seventh knot.

"So mote it be."

Thank Divinity, then wrap your cord around the item. Place in a safe place until the person is healed. Then hold your hands over the cord, thank Divinity again, and slowly undo each knot, saying:

"Blessings upon myself and my loved ones. So mote it be."

Second spell ~ Pennsylvania Dutch healing spell

German-American folk magick consisted of saying a variety of chants. This one is said nine times a day until the individual is well. As a friendly Amish Witch once told me, you didn't get sick in a day, so don't expect to get well in a day.

Hold a picture of the sick person in your hand, and concentrate on that person. Say the person's full name first. Then, repeat these spell words:

"I saw a green wall.
Through the green wall I saw a green sanctuary.
In the green sanctuary I saw a green altar.
On the green altar I saw a green bowl.
In the green bowl I saw clear water.
I picked up the water and WASHED out the infection!
So mote it be!"

As you say "washed," visualize pure, healing waters running over the person's picture. Finish this spell by making the sign of the equal-armed cross (see page 45) over the picture. Put the picture in a safe place and repeat nine times each day until the person is well. Never give up.

Tuesday ~ war day spells

The planet Mars rules this day, helping to make it a day of male energy, aggression, challenges, and action.

On Tuesday, work magick related to these issues:

Overcoming obstacles/problems, meeting challenges (especially by taking action), the element of Fire, self-esteem issues, beginnings, athletics, issues related to men, other people's money, tools, healing from accidents, and any type of craftsmanship/working with your hands, especially with a view to "making things go." Police and soldiers are covered by this fiery energy. Think before you speak, and use that action energy to get things done in a positive way. If a friend or relative works in a field such as law enforcement, this is a great day to work on a little protection magick.

Spells to boost self-esteem

Perhaps the biggest challenge of all in life is raising our self-esteem. So many people are eager to grind us under their heels, usually so that they can raise their own poor self-esteem. Who am I and what do I want to be? Everyone asks these kinds of questions, and if we're a bit depressed, we often push them to one side, or escape into drugs, alcohol, or apathy. These two spells are great if you're feeling blue about yourself.

First spell—putting together your magickal journal

Spend a Tuesday putting together your Book of You. Be sure to have the kind of book you can add to throughout the year, such as a large scrapbook. Make it as decorative as you like. Include pictures of yourself, a list of ten people you admire and why (judge them by quality, not by their looks or what they own), a list of things you are good at, a list of things you like to do, and a list of what you would like to do with your future. On the last page of your book, write: "Small Acts of Kindness."

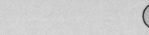

Second spell ~ working with your good points

Self-esteem is all about how you see yourself. If we learn to see ourselves in a positive way, then we have a greater chance of being the best that we can be, which in turn reinforces our good self-image.

You will need:

* Paper and a pen
* A picture of you
* The magickal pouch/a piece of black cloth
* The silver bell

Sit down and write out a GREAT BIG list of all the good things about yourself. Then copy them onto the back of a picture of yourself. Next, make a list of the things in yourself you would like to improve. Put those on the picture of yourself, too. Do not write down negative things that people say about you that

you may have internalized, and now believe. For example, no one is ugly. We can all do things to improve our appearance, but remember that every single person has at least one stunning feature.

Wrap the picture in your magickal kit pouch (or a piece of plain black cloth) and put it in your dresser drawer. Once a day for the next seven days, stand in front of a mirror and repeat the following chant while staring into your eyes:

"Aries Fire and cardinal dance,
Wake within me tender glance.
Inner beauty I bring to fore,
I bless the day that I was born.
Within this mirror I'm glad to see
Truth be told, that love is me."

Ring your silver bell three times, saying:

"I ward off any negativity. Keep me safe. Keep me free. So mote it be."

Keep the picture hidden away. When you feel down, hold the picture in your hands and repeat the spell. Update your pictures, and lists, at least once a year.

Spell for courage

It isn't easy to be strong. Sometimes it is so tough we're not sure we can make it—but we do. If you need a bit of courage, then the Aries Moon might have that extra oomph you require. In the Zodiac the animal symbol for courage is Leo, the stately, regal lion, so you need a picture of a lion for this spell. Now, this isn't a spell to use if someone is daring you to do something. We're too smart for that because we know that when people dare us to do something, they are really trying to control our behavior (since they aren't very good at controlling their own). A dare is a bullying tactic, and Witches don't go there! This spell is designed to help us when we need to tell the truth about something, or face our friend and tell him or her that we don't do drugs—that kind of courage.

You will need:

❊ A picture of a lion
❊ A red pencil
❊ A rubber band

Take the picture of the lion and wrap it tightly around a red pencil. Secure with a rubber band. Hold the pencil in your hands, and say:

"Every action has a reaction.
Every problem has a solution.
Every thought can be manifest.
The courage of the lion in me.
Yesterday, today, and tomorrow.
So mote it be!"

Say the spell as many times as it takes for you to believe it! Keep the pencil with you to fill you with courage, and renew the spell every thirty days until you no longer feel you need help.

Wednesday ~ communication day spells

This is chatterbox/fast communication day. The planet Mercury rules Wednesday, and Mercury's male energy is that of a messenger. All sorts of messages, telephone calls, and e-mails bounce around. In business, Wednesday is called "hump day," meaning it is halfway through the work week. Many career people try to get as much done on Wednesday as possible—it's much better than Mondays or Fridays, when people are either recovering from the weekend or getting ready to cut loose.

On Wednesday, work magick related to these issues:

Any type of communication and learning: studying for a test, writing a school paper, trying to find someone, making new friends (and keeping old ones), working with the element of Air, planning a project, finding a job in the field of communications, or making a decision. Mercury also rules siblings and people in your life that you don't know too well (the postman, one of your parent's friends, etc.) and short-distance travel.

Taking care of business

All too often we forget to say "thank you" and "sorry." Wednesday's quicksilver energy makes it a good day to take care of such loose communication ends. Send a card, make an apologetic phone call, and ask the element of Air to enhance your conversation. Wednesday is "Honest Day"—be true to yourself and those around you. Vehicles for Air magick include incense, paper airplanes, fans, breathing exercises, and even storms.

Spell for better communication

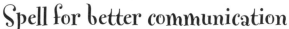

Wednesday's energy focus is the retrieval or transmission of information. It encompasses the energy of both conveying and listening. The art of communication is hard to master. One of the greatest skills you can ever attain is really listening to others—and then speaking appropriately, at the right time.

Go to the tree or wherever you plan to tie your ribbons. Hold the ribbons in your hands and ask that the element of Air bless the ribbons and bring you the ability to listen to others, understand what they say, think logically about your response, and communicate in a clear and concise manner. As you tie each ribbon on the tree or fence, repeat your request:

You will need:

* A tree, post, or fence outside
* Seven colored ribbons

"May I receive the ability and patience to listen to others.
May I understand what they say.
May I think logically about my responses.
May I communicate in a clear and concise
manner. As the Air of the universe moves
these ribbons, my wishes will be granted.
So mote it be."

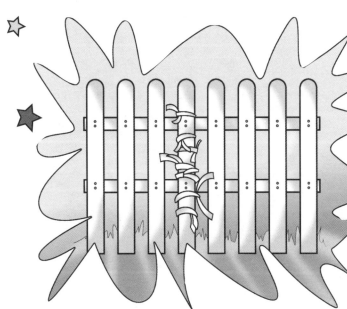

Leave the ribbons where you have tied them. Don't worry yourself if someone comes along and takes them. Once the magickal operation has left your hands, your desire for change has already reached Spirit. The energy dance has begun and no one can stop it!

Spell for doing that homework

Studying can be a delight or a chore. Studying well depends on your interests, time allowance, personal needs, and yes ... even your self-esteem. What makes studying so hard is that not everyone learns in the same way. Choose what system works best for you, and don't start to believe people if they say you are stupid, as that will only block your ability to learn.

Now for the spell. Hold your hands over your homework books and papers, and say:

"Help me study three times three.
Bring me joy and harmony.
Don't forget the clarity—
Patience, knowledge, and privacy.
I call the flow of Air energy.
Help me study three times three.
I seal this spell,
So mote it be!"

Now blow on your homework nine times.

The why and how of studying

Why bother to study? When school is over, won't that be the end of learning stuff? No. It's the beginning! Throughout your life you will end up studying all manner of things— from learning to ski to looking after a pet. Almost everything you do, if it's worth doing, will require learning something new. The ball is always in your court; whether you choose to play, foul, or quit is entirely up to you.

If you must study something that you have no interest in, be kind to yourself. Think about how you like to learn things. Perhaps you could rent a video, surf the internet, visit a historical site, etc. Expand your studies with related topics that do interest you. Find a spot where you can concentrate and study in short bursts to help your retention. Chewing spearmint gum or drinking spearmint tea is said to enhance memory retention.

Spell for protection for short-distance travel

You will need:

* The magickal pouch or a small blue or silver bag
* A teaspoon of rosemary (from the grocery store)
* A seashell
* A symbol of the God/dess or deity of your choice

We all worry about traveling out there on the road (or rails). Here's a spell to work protective magick for yourself, your friends, and relatives. Take your pouch/bag and place inside it the rosemary, the shell, and the symbol. Tie it securely. Hold the bag in your hands and concentrate on you and the vehicle in question being protected by something you think is strong—angels, polar bears, whatever. Renew every three months.

Spell for giving a speech or performing

Whether you are in school or college, there comes a time when you will need to give a presentation or a speech. How you present yourself has a lot to do with how people perceive you. If they don't like what they see, they won't listen to what you have to say.

Keep smiling ...

You might have to dress up a little. Talk to people like you are speaking to your best friend. If you mess up, keep smiling and keep going. If they make fun of you, make a joke about it or ignore them. Preparation is key. Have your notes ready, know the material forward and backward, use props, and be sure to add something interactive for the audience to do. Speak clearly, smile—and use a little magick.

You will need:

* A small, clean bottle
* Perfume or aftershave
* Water
* A handkerchief (cotton is better than paper)

In the bottle, mix one half-teaspoon of perfume/aftershave with one teaspoon of water. Sprinkle the mixture onto the handkerchief, saying the following words at the same time:

"Glamoury, at birth you be
the substance of poise and dignity."*

*Glamoury is a type of illusion

Repeat the incantation nine times. Allow the cloth to dry. Repeat the chant the night before the presentation. On the day, have the hankie in your pocket. Just before the presentation, take a deep breath, ground, center, and smile. Smell the cloth and think of yourself surrounded by poise. Walk forward with your head up, smiling. Imagine Spirit entering the top of your head and filling your body with calm, relaxing energy. Now go! (And save the cloth for the next presentation.)

Spell for perfecting an idea

This simple spell requires just a regular deck of cards. Separate the cards into four suits. If your idea is about emotions, choose the suit of hearts. If you want to focus on communication and daily tasks, use clubs. For money, property, and education issues, choose diamonds. Use spades only to banish illness. By learning to use the four suits, you can tailor this spell to any project, issue, or problem in your life. Just reword the spell slightly to fit your circumstances. After you choose the appropriate suit, lay the cards out from Ace to King, saying the following as you go:

*"Ace: This is the beginning of the idea.
Two: This is the partnership between myself and Spirit.
Three: This is the research or skill I will learn to accomplish my goal.
Four: This is the firm root system that will help me succeed.
Five: This is the process of change that must occur.
Six: This is my experience that will help me as I move ahead.
Seven: This is my strength to overcome any challenge.
Eight: This is growth that will occur as the result of my goal.
Nine: This is my promise for success.
Ten: This is the positive fulfillment of my desires.
Jack: This is all the messages and information that I need to reach my goal.
Queen: This is the Goddess that nurtures my idea and ensures that my goal is part of my life plan.
King: This is the God that protects my desire, gives me structure, and supports my life path."*

Spell to understand how to be good to others

You will need:

❖ Seven buttons

❖ A sturdy piece of string or yarn that will fit through the buttonholes

Virgo's Earth energy brings stability and compassion to any spell involving service to others. Cleanse and consecrate the buttons and ask your chosen deity to bless them. When the Moon is in Virgo, string the buttons, and say as you do so:

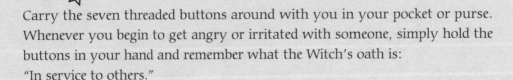

"Button, one button ~ I call forth universal love.
Button, two buttons ~ I call forth universal compassion.
Button, three buttons ~ I call forth logic.
Button, four buttons ~ I call forth fairness.
Button, five buttons ~ I call forth equality.
Button, six buttons ~ I call forth the Great God.
Button, seven buttons ~ I call forth the Gracious Goddess.
Buttons, all buttons be blessed in service, be blessed in honor; be blessed in courage.
Buttons, all buttons be the girdle of the Goddess [tie the two ends of the string or yarn together].
Honor is the law.
Love is the bond.
So mote it be."

Carry the seven threaded buttons around with you in your pocket or purse. Whenever you begin to get angry or irritated with someone, simply hold the buttons in your hand and remember what the Witch's oath is: "In service to others."

Spell to find the missing detail

You will need:
* A sheet of white paper
* A pen or pencil

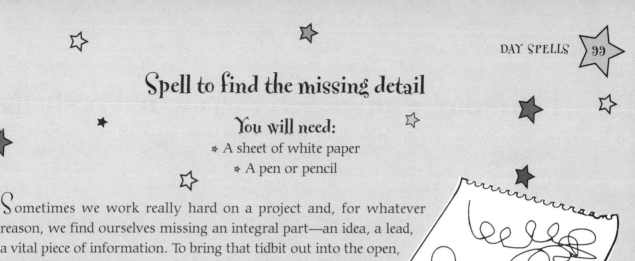

Sometimes we work really hard on a project and, for whatever reason, we find ourselves missing an integral part—an idea, a lead, a vital piece of information. To bring that tidbit out into the open, try this simple spell.

Draw a small circle in the center of the paper. This is the hidden information. Around the edges of the paper, start to doodle. Take your time. Let the pen or pencil move any which way. Slowly work toward the circle in the center. As you draw, relax and let go of worries and tensions. Let the pen, the drawing, and your mind become one.

When most of the paper is completely filled with your design, draw one last line that connects the circle with the rest of the work. At the moment the line reaches the edge of the circle, say: "I have found the answer." In the center of the circle, draw the symbol for the planet Mercury (☿)

Hang the paper up where you can see it clearly (on a bulletin board, bedroom mirror, etc.) Very soon that illusive fact or piece of information will make itself known to you—perhaps in a random conversation with a friend, or through a TV show, or whatever.

Thursday ~ money and growth day spells

Thursday comes under the expanding motion of Jupiter—the big, fat planet of more, more, more, but with a good dose of kindness, humanitarianism, and humor thrown in.

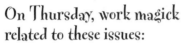

On Thursday, work magick related to these issues:

Jupiter is associated with money, lending, matters of expansion, legal issues, things that benefit you, higher education or classes you take outside of regular school classes/work, and also with planning for your future. Other Jupiter issues include favors, spirituality, religion, and physicians. This is the day to add new ideas to something that you've already been working on, to open up a new bank account (especially over the New Moon phase and particularly a savings account), or to work toward a fixed, financial goal (like saving money to buy something big). Be expansive in your kindness. Try researching new religions and cultures.

Spell to bring you a few extra pennies

You will need:
* Some coins
* A large, flat stone
* Some perfume or aftershave

You are not the sum of your money and possessions. That aside, everyone could use a little prosperity! Ask Spirit or a deity (the Greco-Roman Juno works well for money) to bless all the items you have gathered together. Arrange the coins in a circle on the stone. Pour three drops of perfume in the center of the circle. Ask Spirit to bring abundance into your life in a positive way. Repeat this spell for seven days, once a month—it's best to begin on a Thursday when the Moon is waxing.

Spell for overall prosperity

You will need:

* Seventy-five pennies
* A bottle of spring water (from the grocery store)
* The Earth quartz crystal

Keep in mind that prosperity is an energy, not a physical thing when working money magick. Use this spell as part of a long-term financial plan. Ask Spirit to bless the pennies and the water. Over the sink, to avoid making a mess, slowly drop the pennies in the water. If the bottle opening isn't large enough, put the water into another container. The water will come out the top and go into the sink. That's okay. As you drop in each penny, say:

"I immerse this penny in the waters of prosperity. I open myself to the positive abundance of the universe. Each penny draws blessings to me."

After you have filled the bottle with the pennies, cap the bottle/container, dry it, hold it in your hands, and repeat the spell. Name the item for which you need added prosperity (a college fund, CD player, or book, for example). Find a place in your room where the bottle won't be disturbed. Place your crystal on top of the bottle and ask that the spirits of Earth assist in bringing you what you need. Keep the bottle in your room (unopened) until your desire manifests. If you are saving for something big, then repeat the words of the spell while holding the bottle each Moon in Taurus until your desire has manifested.

Remember that you will need to work toward your goal in other ways, too. For example, if you are saving up for a CD player, you will also need to look around for the right make and model, choose the best time to purchase, and so on.

The money magnet spell

You will need:

* The golden prosperity coin
(or make one out of gold foil)
* Some oil (preferably sandalwood)
* Some green paper or cloth
* The golden wish cord
* The kit altar

Place a small dot of oil on each face of the coin.
Wrap the coin in the green paper or cloth and secure with your
wish cord. Place the coin in the center of your altar with the wish cord hanging off the edge
toward you. Slowly pull the coin toward you, saying:

"Earth and sea, sky and fire
Prosperity is my desire.
Money come and money grow
This is my wish and now it's so!"

Pull the cord slowly toward you. Keep your magick "money
magnet" coin in your pocket or purse.

Spell/invocation to call upon Divinity

Learning to widen our horizons is very important. Thursday is a perfect day to get to know who or what we think runs the universe. It is vital that we have a good relationship with Spirit so that we can count on help when things get tough.

Invoking Divinity brings Spirit into the circle and perhaps directly into you, to guide you. There is nothing weird about this; you will not be possessed by the Devil. This is a different kind of energy altogether, where you and Spirit become one with the universe. If you have cast your circle, called your quarters, and carry love and honor in your heart, nothing bad can happen. While you are learning it might be easier to simply invite Spirit into your circle, rather than give it a name. Be polite. Divinity is, after all, bigger than us.

I have provided the following three invocations, written by David Norris, for you to try in your own rituals or ceremonies. Before saying the invocation, put a dab of sandalwood oil in the middle of your forehead, think of universal love, and imagine white light cleansing your body. You can actually use these on any day of the week, and in any magickal working, with great success.

Invocation to Spirit (using a white candle):

"Come, eternal Spirit, enter
From your starry cosmic shore.
Bring the fire of bright creation,
Open wide your magick door.
In between the worlds I gather,
Descend in love and harmony.
Fill my heart with hope and wisdom,
Hear my sacred call to thee.
And as you will
So mote it be."

Invocation to the Goddess (using a silver candle):

"Goddess, sweet and sacred Mother,
O seedbed of the world's creation,
Changing Woman, crone, and maiden,
Shadow and bright lightning's fire,
Fill my heart and join my hands
In the working of this hour.
Enter Mother, welcome Goddess!"

Invocation to the God (using a gold candle):

"Father, ancient and eternal,
Stag and warrior of the world,
O spark of life whose animation
Stirs the heart of sacred Mother.
Join me in this mystic working
Father, consort, and protector,
Hear my call and welcome be!"

A question of color

Note that colors (for example colors of candles) are used in some day spells that don't always tie in with the colors of the week given on page 84. This is because I have found that other colors work better in certain spells. Stick to the colors suggested within the spells or experiment with day-of-the-week colors – be creative!

★ Friday ~ love day spells

This is the day filled with the feminine energies of Venus—the ultimate goddess of love, pleasure, and beauty who also rules matters of wealth and success. Venus works well with both Earth and Air energies. Add an element of gentle, serene, yet passionate Venus to any spell that involves your relationship with either an object or a person. As Friday chugs into the weekend, the energies for this day are laid back and smooth, tinged with the excitement of the weekend to come. Go for it!

On Friday, work magick related to these issues:

Anything that falls in the realm of love, pleasure, and relationships, and that may include building a relationship with anyone—a friend, boy/girlfriend, relative, or teacher. And beauty, art, music, manners, flowers, restaurants, new clothing—all fall under the control of a Venus day. Friday is the day for matters to do with fast cash, wealth, and success funneled through the things that you own. Venus also rules teamwork issues, so choose a Friday to turn to her (or Saturn) if, for example, you felt that you were being unfairly targeted.

On a Friday, concentrate on being nice to yourself as well as to others and on seeking serenity. This is a great time to look for a passive, peaceful place to do some of that thinking and relaxing that are so important for any growing mind (young or old). Find a place that really feels like it is just for you—a corner will do! Decorate your magickal place with pictures from magazines, postcards, or your own drawings. If your parents say it's okay, you could build a small circle with stones in your yard. Place offerings to your chosen deity inside the circle, or sit beside it and just dream. If you simply can't find anywhere, make a place in your head—a special, magickal place where you can retreat.

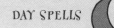

Spell for ready cash

*H*ere's a simple one. If you're a bit down on your luck financially, inscribe a green candle with the symbol of Venus, asking Spirit to help line your pocket with a little ready cash.

Spell/meditation for love and power

You will need:

* A flower
* Your kit altar
* One or two rose-pink candles
* Incense in a holder

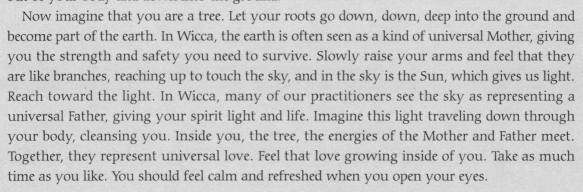

Place the flower in the center of your altar. If you are allowed to have candles and incense, light both and place to the side of the altar. Then sit or stand and close your eyes. Take ten deep breaths in through your nose and out through your mouth. Allow yourself to relax. Imagine any negative feelings draining out of your body and down into the ground.

Now imagine that you are a tree. Let your roots go down, down, deep into the ground and become part of the earth. In Wicca, the earth is often seen as a kind of universal Mother, giving you the strength and safety you need to survive. Slowly raise your arms and feel that they are like branches, reaching up to touch the sky, and in the sky is the Sun, which gives us light. Reach toward the light. In Wicca, many of our practitioners see the sky as representing a universal Father, giving your spirit light and life. Imagine this light traveling down through your body, cleansing you. Inside you, the tree, the energies of the Mother and Father meet. Together, they represent universal love. Feel that love growing inside of you. Take as much time as you like. You should feel calm and refreshed when you open your eyes.

Spell for inner beauty

Meditations like this and the last can be used whenever you don't feel like going through all the preliminaries or casting a circle and so on. Just perform the meditation and ask for solutions or whatever to come to you.

The Inner Beauty Spell requires a nice seashell, but if you don't have one, use a canning jar. Here, you are going to learn how to overcome "Mr./Ms. Negative" (that nagging voice in your head telling you that you're not good enough). This person has been created from your fears—well, we aren't going to let our fears get the better of us!

Choose one positive goal—say, you want to pass an algebra test—and repeat that goal (speaking into the seashell or the jar). Put the shell (or jar) to your ear. If Mr./Ms. Negative says something mean, ignore it and speak the goal again. Repeat the process until Mr./Ms. Negative minds their manners and you only hear a positive response in your head. Weed out all those negative associations you have about yourself and then give your goal a go. You might fail, but at least try—trying and overcoming fears is what life is all about.

Spell to find good friends

You will need:

* A cup
* The kit altar
* Incense in a holder
* The silver bell
* Some brown sugar
* A plastic bag

For pagans, to raise a cup (a "chalice" in pagan terms) in the air is to salute Spirit and wish for good health, or it is a way to ask Spirit to witness an oath. Couples drink from the same cup as a symbol of togetherness. The cup has long been a symbol of Water, emotion, love, and change. Use it here to good effect and make your friendships prosper.

In this simple spell we use the symbolism of the cup to promote energies of friendship and love. Place the empty cup in the center of your altar. Light some incense and ring your silver bell three times. Use an appropriate invocation to mark the beginning of this friendship working. Sprinkle a teaspoon of brown sugar into the cup. As you hold your hands over the cup, say in your own words what you are looking for in love or friendship. Don't mention a person by name, as that is considered to be messing with their free will. For example, "Please make Cynthia like me" is borderline trouble. Instead, you could word this part of the spell in this manner:

"Spirit, I have been having trouble making friends lately. No one seems to like me. If I am doing something that is morally wrong, or behaving in an inappropriate manner, please give me the skills to learn how to work better with the people around me. If I am behaving in the right way, please send clarity and understanding to me so that I may work through the challenges I am experiencing with people. Please move negative people and negative energies away from me. If I am to learn a lesson, please help me see what that lesson is supposed to be. So mote it be."

Hold your hands over the cup until they begin to feel warm or tingle. Now, sit patiently, close your eyes, and let your thoughts wander, allowing Spirit time to help you work out any difficulties, or finish the spell by putting the brown sugar in a plastic bag. Sprinkle the brown sugar around your locker at school, or at the doors of where you work. You can also sprinkle it on the doorstep of your home.

Putting the spell to other uses

The cup in this spell stands for the feminine divine and, most of all, for transformation, so you can tailor this spell to other needs. For example, if someone is ill, you can put their picture in the cup and sprinkle the brown sugar over the photograph. Place the picture and the sugar in a plastic bag, and put it away where it will not be touched. When the sick person is well, scatter the brown sugar to the winds and put the picture back in your photo album.

Saturday ~ day of endings spells

Saturday represents the finish line in magick work: endings, making things go away, protecting yourself against negative actions, people, and energies, following the rules, learning to work within guidelines, and so on. Saturday is ruled by Saturn, the planet of constraint, rules, and closure, yet it is not a negative planet. Some rules are good—too much freedom can be as bad as too many rules. Saturn helps us to balance our lives, be responsible, and make sure that things don't get out of hand. In astrology, formidable Saturn rules Capricorn and Aquarius, and presides over the tenth house—where you decide what you want to be when you grow up.

On Saturday, work magick related to these issues:

Define goals, plan term papers, remove (in a positive way) people from your life who you know aren't good for you, get rid of bad habits, magickally cleanse your room, practice magick for wisdom, plan a trip or adventure, study, investigate every angle of a problem … you get the picture.

Saturday is the day to work on banishing addictions—from drugs to shopping. It is also the day to stick up for others or for the values that you know are right. You'll get a chance to deal with all of these issues on a Saturday, as this is when teens get together to have fun! If your friends try to tempt you into dangerous habits, remember that the only power they have over you is the power you give them. And the feelings of control that addictions give you are an illusion. Look within yourself and find the courage to walk away from dependency-related problems. If your friend is drunk—don't get in that car. Call your parents or another friend.

Although spellwork can enhance the process of dealing with addiction problems, it can't solve them. Always seek professional help—whether it affects you or others (check out the hotlines in the back of this book). You have a long and prosperous life ahead of you—make the most of it!

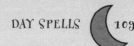

Spells to banish negativity and problems

The first spell ~ asking Spirit for help

This spell is very easy. Sit in a quiet place and ask Spirit for courage and for advice about planning wisely for your future. If you have an addiction, ask for strength to deal with it. Every Saturday, stand facing West, and say: 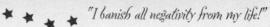 *"I banish all negativity from my life!"*

Although this sounds like a simple procedure, you would be amazed how your life will turn around just by doing this every Saturday for a whole month! It can't solve all your problems at a stroke, but it's a great start. Write a list of what you want to remove from your life, and burn that list each Saturday as you physically work toward removing bad habits. Ask the energy of Saturn, the guardian, to help you in your work.

The second spell ~ tanglefoot spell

You will need:

* Three new sewing needles
* A spool of black thread
* Some black cloth or paper
* The kit altar
* The silver bell

This very effective spell is not to be used directly on a person, but rather to tangle up any negativity around you. Then, through your removal of the "tanglefoot," you push unwanted energies out of your life. Arrange the needles carefully on a flat surface. First, cross one needle over another so that it looks like you have a needle "X." Carefully begin weaving the black thread around the two needles, keeping the "X" shape.

When you think the "X" will hold, very slowly push the third needle down through the thickness of thread in the center of the other two. Your needles will look like a funny bird's foot. Continue weaving the thread around all three needles until you are sure that the whole thing will hold.

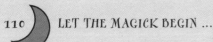

Put some black cloth or paper over your kit altar and place the tanglefoot on top. Hold your hands over your altar and say:

"Powerful winds and shining sea
Catch the negativity.
Nothing evil can float about
Tangles caught, they can't get out."

Repeat the charm nine times, ringing your silver bell before each repetition. After the last time, ring the bell and say: *"So mote it be."*

Take the tanglefoot and bury it outside, off your property. As you lay it into the ground, say:

"Buried now you will be
Never to harm my family or me.
So mote it be."

If things are particularly bad, repeat the spell once a month at the Dark of the Moon until your problems are solved.

Spell to protect your property

This simple spell should be done at the turn of any of the seasons of the year. Take a small amount of salt and walk around the edges of your property in a clockwise direction three times. As you pass your front door, throw a bit of salt from your kit (or any salt you have). As you pass by your back door, throw a bit more salt. As you pass by the largest window, drop the rest of the salt. While you walk, repeat the following three words in succession: *"Patience, Power, Protection."*

When you have finished, walk to the center of the property and ask that Spirit protect your dwelling and those who reside within.

Sunday ~ success day spells!

Sunday is the ultimate day of success for any project or venture, and it is ruled by the courageous, powerful energy of the Sun. Think of sunshine cutting through the veil of confusion, the golden glow of doing something right and the feeling of harmony when you are at a family gathering and everything is moving along in a loving way. The energy of the Sun works well in almost any type of magickal activity you might wish to plan.

In astrology, the Sun rules the courageous male-energy sign of Leo and sits catlike in the fifth house of pleasures, covering things like goals, leadership responsibilities, creativity (art, dance, photography, theater, etc.) and passions for things you love to do (reading, horseback riding, being in the school play). The Sun also stands for benevolent authority figures—those people who are kind and powerful at the same time.

On Sunday, work magick related to these issues:

Sunday is definitely a creative day and a day for doing something that you've procrastinated about (yes, that includes straightening up your room!). Make a commitment on Sunday that every time you start to waste time, you'll think of something else you've been putting off—and do it! Prioritize things. Make plans. Set goals. Write your personal mission statement—this says what you want to accomplish in the next year, and in your lifetime. You can change your mission statement as you grow older. It evolves just like you do.

Spell for making lists come true!

Make a list of the things you must do, remembering to add some fun things. Set your list in the Sun and ask for the energy of Fire and success! When you finish all your tasks, tear the paper up and throw it away. Thank Spirit for helping you accomplish your work and your play.

Spells for manifesting something made by your own hands

Many artists will tell you that their best work blossoms from difficult periods in their lives. By being creative (even if we feel we are untalented) we manifest harmony and ease strain. So find an artistic outlet for your stress and give it a go on a Sunday. The Moon in Leo is a great time for the arts (though Moon in Libra and Pisces are good, too). Here are some spells to enhance creativity, but you can also use them for daily tasks such as homework.

1. Burn a white candle while working and ask Spirit to bless you with creativity. If you are not permitted to burn candles, think of pure white light surrounding your work area.

2. Hold your hands over your tools before you begin working. Ask Spirit to fill your mind and hands with creative potential, and bless the work so that it gives pleasure in the future—to yourself and others. Cleanse and consecrate the items with fragrant incense or sprinkle with holy water.

3. Ask your guardian angel aloud to help you when you get stuck.

4. Before you begin work, find what I call the "still point"—a feeling when all is quiet and you are in tune with the universe. Repeat this if you feel the work is getting off track.

5. Read poetry or an inspirational passage from your favorite author or playwright before you begin. You can also do this during the creative process.

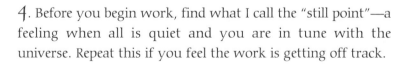

Spell to develop a balanced personality

We all have difficulties in our lives—this is the nature of the learning and growing process. If you feel that things are a little out of whack, try this technique. This magickal working is called a Seven-Day Spell. Seven is considered a magickal number that corresponds with all sorts of mystery teachings.

For this spell, you will need two pieces of paper—one white and one black. Cut the same size circle out of each bit of paper. Now cut the circles in half. Tape a white half and a black half together to make one complete circle. Do not tape the other two halves together just yet.

On the first day that you perform the spell, put the taped circle in the middle. Place a picture of yourself on top. Say the word "Balance" seven times while you hold your hand over your picture.

To the right of the picture, about seven inches away, place either the black or white half of the circle that you have left. It doesn't matter which half you choose. On the left side of the central circle, also seven inches away, place the other half paper circle. The straight edge of the cut circles should face the whole circle in the center.

Moving closer

Each morning and evening, hold your hands over your picture and repeat the word "Balance" seven times, then move both half circles closer to the center. On the last day, put the halves on top of your picture and tape the two halves together, again repeating the word "Balance" seven times. You now have a balanced sandwich, with you in the middle!

Tape the new circle to the old one, keeping your picture in the center. Place this balanced sandwich in your Book of Shadows, your Bible, or other book that is out of sight and out of mind of others. Renew every six months, on your birthday, or simply when you feel like it.

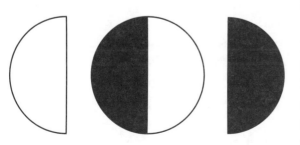

Spell to learn to be a gracious leader

It is incredibly hard to learn to be a gracious leader because our own desires, feelings, and thoughts sometimes get in the way. Trying to be fair to everyone all the time is a tall order! The best we can do is to focus on what we know in our hearts is the right way to behave.

You will need:
- One large orange
- A tablespoon of gold glitter
- The magickal pouch (or another cloth bag if you are using it for other things)

Cut the orange in half. Hold your hands over the orange pieces and say:

*"Courage, will, and generosity
Gracious leader I will be.
Raven wing and earthly tree,
I rise and work for unity.
So mote it be."*

Sprinkle the glitter on both orange halves, repeating the words twice more. Set the orange halves on the windowsill of your room. Slowly, they will begin to dry. Each day, hold your hands over the orange halves and repeat the incantation. When the halves have completely dried (this may take a few weeks, depending on the area in which you live), crush them and place them in your pouch or bag. Carry the bag with you. Re-empower the bag six months later. Renew the following year if you so desire.

There we are. The week is over – and look how much magick you've done!

How to write your own spells

Did you know that you can write a great spell or ritual all by yourself? When *Teen Witch* came out, curious reporters would call me for an interview, and they inevitably asked me the same question—where did the spells in the book come from? When I answered, truthfully, that my daughters and I made them up, most of the reporters snorted or laughed, and one or two got downright nasty. They just couldn't conceive that if you know various magickal correspondences (what goes with what) and timings (such as the days and the Moons), then the opportunities for writing your own spells were endless—and your own spell will pack more punch than one written by someone else because you created it personally.

The rules are few:

- Think before you leap. Be serious. Sit down, think about it thoroughly, and plan it carefully—perhaps write a list of priorities, or make a visual plan (see next page)

- Do your research—thoroughly.

- Be honorable and honest in your proceedings.

- Think hard about the goal that you want to achieve and about all the possible results of your spell—it should do no harm.

- Remain focused throughout.

- Don't work while you are angry or stressed—cool off and get a clear head.

- Always try to mix magick and the regular world together. If you want to pass your driver's test, you will also need to study.

- Don't forget Spirit—that's the most important part.

- Never say never. Think positively. Negative thoughts will wreck your work.

- Use your head—it all starts there.

A few final points. Always analyze your part in the magick. Before wand hits air, ask yourself just how much of what is happening to you, which makes you want to perform a spell, is directly due to your past actions. Could you change a behavior pattern? In the end, only you can take responsibility for your actions, so take control. A single spell won't solve a problem on its own—you have to put in some hard work of your own, too, to make changes in your life. Here are a couple of effective—and fun—spell-planning techniques. Try them on for size and see what you think.

Dot-to-dot spell planning

Take a big piece of white paper and draw ten big dots on it, anywhere you like. At any old dot write the number one, and beside that number write down the root of the issue. Pick another dot. Make that number two. Who's involved in your particular issue? (If there is more than one person, you can use more than one dot; if it is just you, put your name beside the dot.) Find another dot—any one will do. That's dot number three. Write down how soon you have to have a solution (or when you would like your work to manifest—be easy on yourself; don't give yourself an unreasonable time limit).

Pick dot number four. Write down all the things you have to do in the real world to make this happen. Dot number five is the kind of magick you want to do. Fire magick? Earth? Maybe Air? Perhaps color magick. Your choice. Dot five is the timing. When are you going to do this magick? Are you going to use magickal days, the phase of the Moon ...?

Dot seven represents your magickal supplies. Do you need a candle, a colored pen, water? Again, your choice. Dot number eight is your deity choice. Spirit? The Lord and the Lady? A special Goddess or God? Write that choice beside dot number eight. Dot number nine is the "Did I forget anything?" dot. Look back over what you have written. Did you forget something? Dot number ten is where you write your ultimate goal.

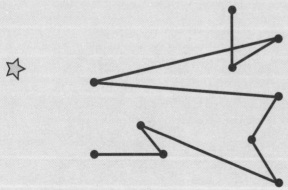

Make the connection

Now, connect the dots, reading everything you have written. The pattern you have made by connecting the dots is your very own magickal symbol (called a sigil). You can carve this symbol on a candle, in the air over the spell supplies—use your imagination. There. You just did something very important—you pre-planned your magickal work!

The magickal map

For those of you who are very creative with the old pen and paper, instead of drawing dots—draw yourself a little map. Use the same steps. For example, you might start at the bottom left-hand edge of your paper and make a little house. Beside the house you would put what the problem is, or what you want to work for, and why. Draw a road from the house and make a pit stop. Here's where you meet the people involved. Draw a road to the next stop, maybe a big clock, and write down how soon you need to get this grand plan finished.

Take a break

Four might be a motel where you rest overnight to check you've got all the things you need. Five could be a drawing representing the kind of magick you want to do. Six is where and when you are going to do this magick. Seven is a stop at a magick store where you'll get your supplies. Eight is deity—perhaps a park with a statue—while nine is the "did I forget anything?" bit and ten is the ultimate goal of your trip.

Use colored pencils, paints, glitter … and have fun! Save the map and follow it while you work out the steps of your spell or ritual. See? Planning was easy and enjoyable—and you thought it would be deadly dull!

Building a magickal maze

Now, if you have a group of friends (or you could do this by yourself) and you want to work magick together, you could actually make a "magickal maze." Build it someplace like your backyard, and go through the maze under the Full Moon. What a great excuse for a slumber party, no matter how old you are!

You can make seven stops in all. Name the stops yourself. At each stop, you could have something to do. For example, stop one: ground and center, then state your intention. At stop two, you light a candle to take with you, again stating your intention. At stop three, you bless yourself with holy water, stating your intention again.

At stop four, address your deity and state your intention. At stop five, do something to raise energy (singing, clapping, dancing). Stop six: relax, meditate and ponder the world around you, again stating your reason for being there. Stop seven, thank deity, ground and center, and leave the maze, confident that your magickal journey will succeed in the regular world. You can make your maze as elaborate (with little Christmas-tree lights) or as simple as you desire. Fun and magick should be synonymous!

When magick fails

Magick, like anything else in the world, is not a perfect science. Sometimes, no matter how strong our desire, or how hard we plan, or how studious we were in our application, our spells or rituals will lay a giant goose egg. That's life. If your magickal application fails, consider the following:

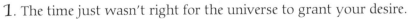

1. The time just wasn't right for the universe to grant your desire.
2. You may have missed something in your spellwork. This is why you should always jot down notes about what you have done, when, where, and why you did it. You might find a loose thread somewhere.

3. Like anything worthwhile, magick takes practice. That's why we're here in the first place—to learn and to succeed. You will not appreciate success if you never fail.

4. One misfired spell does not make a barrel of bad spells. So this one didn't work. Try something different. Maybe you failed simply because you need to learn how to do the same thing many different ways. You can't be perfect all the time—that's not human. Keep your eye on your goal and move forward.

A parting word …

Spells are nothing more than focused prayer combined with your belief in Divinity—there is no mystery. On their own, spells cannot make you lose weight or make Arnie's dad stop hitting him. These situations require real-world solutions. Magick is just a helpful tool. This is not to say that I haven't seen miracles happen, but one must always be pro-active as well as spiritual.

    Magick is in each one of us. As a very special teacher once told me:

"Magick is Love. Dance the dance of the universe in peace and harmony. Learn to bend like the willow, to shine like the Sun, and to love in the name of Spirit. If you achieve that, then you've got it all."

Love,

Silver Raven Wolf
http://www.silverravenwolf.com

Writing to me

★ I am not a certified counselor. If you have a problem, please don't write to me about it. It isn't that I don't want to help you, but, in fairness, I may not be qualified to do so. Instead, talk to your parents or a reliable adult. If you are sick, see a qualified physician.

★ If you are interested in more spells or advanced material, you can get this information from any of Silver's New Generation Witchcraft books (see Useful Books, page 121)

★ Please do write and let me know if this kit has helped you, and if you enjoyed the materials. Always enclose a stamped, self-addressed envelope for my reply, or, if you are living outside of the U.S., an international postage reply coupon. Try to keep your letter to a single page, and allow six months for me to answer you—yes, I get that much mail! I don't answer letters about Satanism or black magick and have no interest in those subjects. Write to me at the following address:

Silver RavenWolf
c/o Llewellyn Worldwide
P.O. Box 64383, K554–1
St. Paul, MN 55164-0383, U.S.A.

Happy Witching!

All you need to know

Useful books

Biedermann, Hans. *Dictionary of Symbolism Cultural Icons and the Meanings Behind Them.* Meridian, New York, NY, 1994.

Forrest, Steven. *Astrology for Beginners—the Inner Sky.* ACS Publications, San Diego, CA, 1988.

Guiley, Rosemary Ellen. *The Encyclopedia of Witches and Witchcraft*, Facts on File, Inc., New York, NY, 1989.

Jones, Alison. *Larousse Dictionary of World Folklore*, Larousse, New York, NY, 1996.

Leach, Maria (Editor). *Funk & Wagnall's Standard Dictionary of Folklore, Mythology, and Legend.* Harper, San Francisco, 1972.

Leek, Sybil. *How To Be Your Own Astrologer.* Cowles Book Company, Inc., New York, NY, 1970.

Mercatante, Anthony S. *The Facts on File Encyclopedia of World Mythology and Legend.* Facts on File, New York, 1988.

Murray, Margarat A. *The God of the Witches.* Oxford University Press, New York, 1970.

Nichols, Ross. *The Book of Druidry.* Thorsons imprint of HarperCollins Publishers, London, 1999 edition, original copyright 1975.

Reid, Lori. *Moon Magick—How to Use the Moon's Phases to Inspire and Influence Your Relationships*, Home

Life, and Business. Three Rivers Press, Crown Publishers, New York, NY, 1998.

Robbins, Rossell Hope. *The Encyclopedia of Witchcraft.* Crown Publishers, New York, NY, 1959.

Walker, Barbara. *The Women's Dictionary of Symbols and Sacred Objects.* Harper, San Francisco, 1988.

Walker, Barbara. *The Women's Encyclopedia of Myths and Secrets*, Harper, San Francisco, 1983.

York, Ute. *Living by the Moon—A Practical Guide for Choosing the Right Time.* Bluestar Communications, Woodside, CA, 1997 (German translation 1993).

And Silver's other books:

All these are published by Llewellyn Worldwide (see page 120 for full address details)
* *Silver's Spells for Protection*, 2000
* *Witches' Night Out* (teen fiction), 2000
* *Silver's Spells for Prosperity*, 1999
* *To Light a Sacred Flame—Book Three New Generation Witchcraft*, 1999
* *Halloween: Customs, Recipes, and Spells*, 1999
* *Teen Witch*, 1998
* *Angels: Companions in Magick*, 1996
* *To Stir a Magick Cauldron—Book Two New Generation Witchcraft*, 1995
* *To Ride a Silver Broomstick—Book One New Generation Witchcraft*, 1993

Hot websites and helplines

Organizations and authors

Raymond Buckland (Author)
    www.geocity.com/soho/workshop/6650
Raven Grimassi (Author) www.Inetworld.net/dgerbe
Robin Wood (Author) www.RobinWood.com
Iron Oak ddi.digital.net/~ironoak
Church of All Worlds www.caw.org/
Ar nDraiocht Fein www.adf.org/
Allegiance of Magickal & Earth Religions
    Carlisle@wuchem.wustl.edu
Pagan Dawn (England) www.paganfed.demon.co.uk
New Moon Rising www.celts.com
Pagan Event Calendar www.io.com
Divine Circle of the Sacred Grove www.grove.org
Temple of the Triple Goddess
    www.geocities.com/Athens/Oracle/8091/index.html or
    members.aol.com/ttgoddess/index.htm
The Bat's N'Bellfrie Zine
    members.tripod.com/~mystweaver
The Celtic Connection www.wicca.com
Crossroads Lyceum/Fellowship of Isis
    members.aol.com/isislyceum/file.html
Crescent Magazine www.crescentmagazine.com
Sage Woman www.sagewoman.com
KC PNO www.candledark.net/PagansNight
Council of Magickal Arts (CMA) www.magickal-arts.org
Witches Voice (Wren and Fritz) www.witchvox.com
Connections www.connections.nu
PagaNet News www.paganet.org

Bookstore and suppliers links

www.magusbooks.com—Magus Books, MN – they can
    find anything
www.bookfinder.com—source for rare, used, or out-of-
    print books
www.bibliofind.com—source for rare, used, or out-of-
    print books
www.goddess.to—on-line store for jewelry, statues,
    aromatherapy oils, and books
www.eldarproductions.com—magickal music
members.aol.com/elvendrums—excellent music and

information on faery magick
www.thecauldron.com—Strange Brew Herbal, Kenmore,
    NY
members.aol.com/MorganasCh—Morganna's Chamber,
    NYC
members.aol.com/cryfox—The Crystal Fox, Laural, MD
www.al.com/wow—World of Wisdom—Indianapolis, IN

Top teen helplines
U.S.

AIDS Helpline 1-800-548-4659
Al-Anon & Alateen 1-800-356-9996
Alcohol & Drug Dependency Hopeline 1-800-622-2255
Boys Town 1-800-448-3000
Bureau of Indian Affairs Child Abuse Hotline
    1-800-633-5133
Child Find of America 1-800-I-AM-LOST
Child Help USA 1-800-422-4453
Child Quest International Sighting Line 1-800-248-8020
Narcotics Hotline 1-800-359-5910
National AIDS Hotline 1-800-342-AIDS
National Clearinghouse for Alcohol & Drug Information
    1-800-SAY-NOTO
National Clearinghouse of Child Abuse and Neglect
    1-800-394-3366
National Cocaine Hotline 1-800-262-2463
National Domestic Violence Hotline 1-800-799-7233
National Institute on Drug Abuse Hotline 1-800-622-HELP
National Referral Network for Kids in Crisis
    1-800-KID-SAVE
National Resource Center on Domestic Violence
    1-800-553-2508
National Respite Locaters Service 1-800-773-5433
National Runaway Switchboard 1-800-621-4000
Rape, Abuse, & Incest National Network 1-800-656-4673
Resource Center on Domestic Violence, Child Protection,
    and Custody 1-800-527-3223
Runaways Hotlines
STD National Hotline 1-800-227-8922

Canada

AIDS Helpline 1-000-518 4659
Alcoholics Anonymous:
   Montreal: 574-866-9803
   Toronto: 416-410-3809
   Vancouver: 604-688-1716
Child Abuse and Neglect 1-800-394-3366
Childline 1-800-668-6868
Domestic Violence 1-800-553-2508
Rape, Abuse, and Incest 1-800-656-4673
Runaway 1-800-621-4000

U.K.

Careline 020-8514-1177
Childline 0800-1111 [Ireland 1-800-666-6666]
Contraceptive Education Service 020-7636-7866
CRUSE 020-8940-3131 (Youth Bereavement Helpline)

Kidscape 020-7730-3300 (help with bullies)
National Association for Children of Alcoholics
   0800-289061
National AIDS Helpline 0345-567123
National Alcohol Helpline 0345-320202
National Drugs Helpline 0800-776600
NSPCC Helpline 0800-800-500
Samaritans 0345-909090

Australia

Al-Anon Australia 03-9654-8838
Australian Federation of AIDS Organizations Information
   Line 1-800-83806
Kids Helpline 1-800-55-1800
Lifeline 13-1114
Narcotics Anonymous (Sydney) 02-9212-3444

Glossary of Wiccan terms

Altar

A surface, usually flat, that is set aside exclusively for magickal workings and is used as a focus of power

Anointing oil

A skin-safe, scented oil that is dabbed on the body (at chosen pulse points or on the forehead) in order to purify an individual mentally and spiritually. You can use anointing oils on your own body, or they may be used during the opening of a ritual on someone who is being invited into the magick circle. As the anointing takes place,

words such as the following are normally spoken:

★ ★ ★ ★ ★

"May you be cleansed, blessed, and regenerated in the name of the Lord and the Lady."

Blue Moon

When there are two Full Moons in one calendar month, the second is called a Blue Moon.

Calling the quarters

Verbal or symbolic acknowledgment of the Four Elements (Earth, Air, Fire, Water) in a ritual environment.

Casting a circle

Creating a mental magickal bubble that encloses the ritual area or an individual (as in protective magick). The circle enhances one's ability to focus, raise power, and contain that power until the person directing the ritual is ready to release the energy. In some practices, the circle is thought to be protective, allowing only the energies you call to enter the circle environment.

Cauldron

An iron pot, of any size, used to prepare ritual magicks, herbals, infusions, and so on. The cauldron is a symbol of the womb and the birth process, the ability to transform oneself into a more

spiritual individual. A three-legged pot is the essence of the Goddess. A four-legged pot brings in the energies of the four quarters (four quarters of the Moon, Four Elements, four compass points, and so on).

Centering

A meditation exercise designed to produce feelings of total calm and one-ness with the universe. It should be preceded by grounding procedures.

Chalice

A cup, made from a variety of materials, that represents the Goddess. It is a symbol of potential.

Circle

See "Casting a circle" and "Esbat."

Clan

Any number of covens who have agreed to follow the same kinds of rules, which spring from one central governing source. A clan has a single leader, and within the democratic clan governing system, he or she has the power to veto proposals or actions.

Correspondence

An item that has a magickal association. Correspondences include: days, planets, stars, monthly Moons, angels, herbs, deities, oils, colors, Zodiac signs, hours, magickal alphabets, divinatory tools such as the Tarot, I-Ching, runes, etc., and many more. If you stick with your magickal

training you will eventually learn all, or most, of these correspondences by heart.

Coven

A small group of people who work together in magick, ritual, and religious activities within the Craft. The traditional number for a coven was thirteen, but covens can be as large as twenty or as few as three individuals.

Crescent Moon

Sacred symbol of the Goddess. Used for sabbats, women's healings, and invocations.

Daily devotions

The practice of acknowledging Deity in your life once or twice every day.

Deity (or Divinity)

Your understanding of a divine spiritual form: Spirit, God/dess or similar.

Deosil (pronounced Jess-el)

Moving in a clockwise direction.

Divination

To foretell the future or check on past or current circumstances by using one's connection to Spirit, one's mind, and a chosen tool (Tarot cards, scrying, I-Ching, runes, astrology, cowrie shells, and so on).

Drawing down the Moon

To connect with Spirit by drawing the power of the Moon into the body, mind,

and spirit, usually during a ritual or a rite. A way of honoring the Goddess.

Eclipse

When one heavenly body obscures another for a short period of time, creating a temporary veil or shadow. For example, a Solar (Sun) eclipse is when the Moon passes between the Earth and the Sun, blotting out some or all of the Sun's light.

Elements

Earth, Air, Fire, and Water. Witches believe also in a fifth element—Spirit.

Empowering

Also called "loading." This means to fill an object with divine energy for a specific magickal purpose or manifestation.

Equal-armed cross

A cross symbol with equally sized arms, used to seal a magickal working.

Esbat

The monthly meeting of Witches to celebrate the Full or New Moon. Most Witches use the term "Circle," rather than Esbat, and many groups meet more than once a month. The meeting is much like the weekly celebrations you might have at a church. A Witch who works alone can hold an Esbat whenever, and as often, as he or she would like. A solitary Esbat can last from fifteen minutes to over an hour. How you plan your ritual is up to you.

God/Goddess

Blanket titles for the universal male and female energy celebrated by the Witches. Together, their combined power equals Spirit.

Grounding

A meditation exercise that allows the mind to focus in a positive way on a specific visualization. To sink excess energy into the Earth or to calm rampant energy in the body. Grounding should be followed by centering procedures.

Holy water

Blessed, purified water for use in ritual. Salt or an herb may be added to the water as part of its ritual purification process.

Invocation

To call Spirit into a circle, ritual, rite, or magickal working.

Lady

Title of honor for the Goddess.

Lord

Title of honor for the God.

Magick

The art and science of focusing your will and emotions to effect change both in the world around you and in the world within you. In itself, magick is neither good nor evil, positive nor negative. It is the use of the power that determines what kind of path it will take.

Meditations

Mental, stress-relieving exercises used to draw body, mind, and spirit into a single focus, in order to enhance the quality of life. Daily meditation practices help to promote a healthier outlook on life and can facilitate healing in the sick.

Moon void of course

An astrological term. At the end of each passage of the Moon through a sign (usually every two or three days) the Moon leaves behind her last aspect (sharing energy with another planet) and prepares to enter a new sign. At this point she is said to be "Void of Course"— that is, without a course, or direction. This stage lasts from a few hours to a few days, during which strange things can happen. Avoid making major decisions or planning important events.

Pentacle

A magickal symbol consisting of a pentagram—a five-pointed star—pointing upward and enclosed by a circle. Worshipped by the ancients, its meaning is "life" or "health." It is worn as a symbol of a Witch's belief and used in magickal workings and ceremonies. Each point on the star relates to the five magickal Elements – Earth, Air, Fire, Water, and Spirit. Pentacles are never worn inverted in the Craft, and to do so is considered blasphemous by many. However, an inverted pentagram is used in some initiations, not to indicate evil but to fulfill a function of growth where one is expected to look within and alter one's bad habits or perspective in order to become a better person.

Pentagram

A magickal symbol, consisting of a five-pointed star.

Phases of the Moon

The stages of our Moon's journey around the Earth. One complete orbit of the Moon around the Earth is called a lunar cycle and takes just under a month. During its journey the Moon passes from New Moon to Full Moon and back to New, going through various stages in between, such as a Crescent Moon. There are eight Moon phases or stages (spread across four quarters) per cycle, and thirteen lunar cycles per year.

Planetary hour

Also called a magickal hour. Divisions of night and day that are guided by astrological influences and the energies of the various planets. Most serious Craft books and astrological texts carry this information.

Quarter call

See "Calling the quarters."

Quarters of the Moon

Astronomical measurement of the Moon's cycle as it journeys around the Earth. The first and second quarters encompass the stages from New to Full Moon, while the third and fourth quarters represent the journey back from Full to New Moon.

Sabbat

A Wiccan Witchcraft ceremony of honor acknowledging the eight segments of the Wiccan year, the cycle of the seasons, and the influence of Spirit in our lives. There are eight Sabbats, also called High Holy Days.

Sacred space

An area cleansed by the four elements and used for religious purposes. You can also create sacred space around your bed if you have trouble sleeping, are in a sick room, and so on.

Sacred spiral

A Wiccan symbol that represents "coming into being"—death and rebirth and the cycle of life. Single and double spirals were among the most sacred signs of Neolithic Europe, and the spiral still plays an important part in magickal workings.

Scrying mirror

A mirror used for divination purposes. It is painted black on one side and dipped or painted with an herbal wash to enhance the power of its reflective surface. The mirror may also feature magickal sigils.

Sigil

A type of symbol. A magically oriented seal, sign, glyph (sculptured character or symbol), or other device used in a magickal working. The most powerful sigils are those that you create yourself. Sigils can be used on

letters, packages, clothing, paper tucked in your pocket ...

"So mote it be"

A much-used expression in WitchCraft. "Mote" means "must" in Old English, so the expression is saying "As I will, it must be done."

Spell

A kind of prayer, spoken or unspoken, that may also use a variety of physical tools (herbs, string, candles, and so on) to help the practitioner's mind to focus on their desire.

Spiral

See "Sacred Spiral."

Spirit

Your personal concept of God/dess – the energy-force that "runs" the universe.

Talisman

An object—a gemstone, a drawing, whatever—that has been magickally charged and is then carried around in order to help the bearer in some way. The charging of the talisman is most important; it can be discharged under running water. The word "talisman" is said to come from the Arabic words *talis ma*, or "magick writing." Talismans work under planetary influences.

Thunder water

An especially potent form of holy water, which is best prepared during a lunar eclipse.

Waning Moon

After a Full Moon, the Moon's shining disk gradually decreases in size as it heads toward the phase called the New Moon. This is known as the period of the Waning Moon, and as the disk decreases, so the Moon's power also fades. This is a good time time for performing banishing magick.

Waxing Moon

As the New Moon makes its journey toward the Full Moon phase, its disk of light grows larger, or waxes. This is a good time for magick that involves growing and building.

Widdershins

Moving in a counterclockwise direction.

Wicca

It is thought that this term was originally coined by Selena Fox of the Circle Sanctuary, in an effort to describe the modern religion of WitchCraft (as begun by Gerald Gardner in England in the 1950s).

Wheel of the Year

One full cycle of the Wiccan year. The year is divided into eight segments or seasons, each of which is marked by a festive celebration (also called a Sabbat). The first such celebration of the year is known as Samhain. This celebratory holiday lasts from October 31 through November 11 and is the Wiccan New Year.

Index

Acknowledgments
Eddison • Sadd Editions

Editorial Director ✤ Ian Jackson
Commissioning Editor ✤ Liz Wheeler
Project Editor ✤ Ann Kay
American Editor ✤ Rebecca Zins
Proofreader ✤ Eleanor Van Zandt
Indexer ✤ Dorothy Frame
Art Director ✤ Elaine Partington
Art Editor ✤ Hayley Cove
Designers ✤ Axis Design
Production ✤ Karyn Claridge, Charles James